More Books Appeal

This book is dedicated
to my loving husband, Thomas E. Gomberg,
who is ever supportive of all my endeavors
and to the memory of my dear Aunt Edith
who will always be with me.
Also, to the memory of each member of the
Cornell family where my roots began.

More Books Appeal

Keep Young Teens in the Library

by
Karen Cornell Gomberg

McFarland & Company, Inc., Publishers
Jefferson, North Carolina, and London

British Library Cataloguing-in-Publication data are available

Library of Congress Cataloguing-in-Publication Data

Gomberg, Karen Cornell.
    More books appeal : keep young teens in the library / by Karen
Cornell Gomberg.
        p.   cm.
    [Includes index.]
    ISBN 0-89950-476-0 (sewn softcover : 50# alk. paper) ∞
    1. Libraries, Young people's — Activity programs.   2. Teenagers —
Books and reading.   3. Youth — Books and reading.   I. Title.
Z718.5.C67   1990
027.8'222 — dc20   89-43619
                                                               CIP

Manufactured in the United States of America

McFarland & Company, Inc., Publishers
  Box 611, Jefferson, North Carolina 28640

TABLE OF CONTENTS

INTRODUCTION

New ideas for school library media center publicity are hard to come by. Many of them have been used already in one form or another. But any idea is new when used in a different place, in a slightly different way, with an audience that has never thought about the library in quite *that* way before. Many of the suggestions in this book are geared toward library publicity and public relations, and they all spring from one idea, not a new one, but the most important idea of all: to make noise, to get attention. Their purpose is not only to encourage student library use, but to make others library-aware: school faculty, board of education members, the superintendent, the administration, parents, and even the public. Let them know the school library is an active, living place, not a stuffy old warehouse.

More Books Appeal is a sequel to *Back to Books: 200 Library Activities to Encourage Reading* (by Karen Marshall) and *Books Appeal: Get Teenagers into the School Library* (by Karen Cornell Gomberg). The volume is a smorgasbord of activities including (1) Publicity; (2) Fun with Book Lists; (3) Quiet Mental Games; (4) Contests and Active Games; (5) Reference Books; and (6) Fiction Crossword Puzzles. Suggestions within these categories often overlap, and consist of various games and activities; banquets, fairs, parties, programs, bazaars, shows, carnivals, tournaments; bulletin boards, posters, displays, projects, exhibits; crossword puzzles; field trips; workshops; clubs; clinics; conventions; productions; awards; notices and commercials; letters; telephone conversations; videotapes; clearinghouses; special days, nights, weeks and months; readathons; deliveries; quizzes; invitations; raffles; lists; swaps; newsletters; fundraisers; questionnaires; and more.

If you can use some assistance enticing your students into the school library media center, and attracting attention to your library, this volume is for you. Pep up your library techniques; perk up your reading program; and "sell" the library! Activate your library programs. Put spirit and spunk into reading and research. Make the library come alive!

The constant use of the library by students, and the number of teachers bringing their classes there, bespeak the success of our library program. The number of books being circulated and the substantial use of reference tools by students also serve as evidence. The activities in this book were found to be effective in our program. Although they are geared for grades 7 and 8, anyone may adapt them for younger or older children. Take off with these ideas on your own. Adapt them to your library, and go on to create more. Enjoy, and have fun!

I. PUBLICITY

1. Treasure Hunt Banquet

Have a treasure hunt banquet. Photocopy entry forms, and place them on the counter beside a deposit box. Students coming into the library media center during this week will have an opportunity to take part in the fun. There will be five questions on the entry forms, some much more complicated than others. The student will write his/her name and the date on the entry form, then research to find the answers in the library media center. The first person or the first five people to answer all questions correctly will win (with the administrator's permission) no homework assignments for three days, plus a pizza.

2. Sweetheart Carnival

Make carnival invitations of red hearts. Decorate the library media center with red and white crepe paper hearts, cupids, and heart stickers. Advertise the party by posters and morning announcements. Individuals or classes may participate in this party.

The object of this activity is for students to match information. For example, one-half of the English class may be given a title of a classic fiction book; the other half, the author's name. Students try to pair titles with authors. Or match book characters with fiction titles, or correlate the activity to any of the subject areas of the curriculum. If half the class is composed of girls, and half boys, divide the class so that girls must match up with boys. Love songs may be softly playing in the background. The winning pair, the pair that comes together the quickest, is the King and Queen of Hearts.

Serve heart-shaped cookies with red and white sprinkles and pink lemonade. Have a cupid's fish pond where students will fish out questions about their topic studied: the elements in chemistry, or whatever. Questions can be devised according to the class. All who answer their questions correctly will be eligible to compete for the title of King and Queen of the Carnival.

3. Lincoln's Party

Decorate the library with photos of Abraham Lincoln, frontier scenes, the Emancipation Proclamation, Civil War photos, and quotations from Lincoln. Hold a debate, discussing opposing viewpoints on political issues. For example, nuclear arms; women's rights; minority rights; capital punishment; euthanasia; AIDS topics; drug abuse; communism; Israel; etc. Students may have a chance to read up on topics selected, and debate individually; or the social studies teacher may assign the class to participate in the debate.

4. Halloween Party

Decorate the library media center with props: spider webs, witches, masks, ghosts, jack-o-lanterns. Hold an apple bobbing contest at the end of the day for students. Whoever gets the apple wins a nice prize. Exhibit books and book lists on supernatural and horror stories. Show a video on the supernatural.

5. A March Wind Party

This event may be in order for a dreary March day or two. Post an exhibit or bulletin of important March events; there are many of them. For example, Ohio became the seventeenth state on March 1, 1803; American poet Robert Frost was born on March 26; and Albert Einstein was born on March 14. Place on the bulletin board some lists of popular beliefs and superstitions about March. The science class, studying aerodynamics, may find appropriate materials. The foreign language class may find "windy words" in dictionaries.

6. *A George Washington Party*

During George Washington week, have a party! Decorate the library media center with photos of George Washington, exhibits of the Declaration of Independence, and scenes of Valley Forge, crossing the Delaware, Mount Vernon, etc. Have a "Cannot Tell a Lie" (true-false) question contest for any class participating. For example, the English class may be asked questions regarding a novel studied, or the foreign language class may be asked the meanings of French words. Those answering correctly are safe; those answering incorrectly are thrown out of the game. The last person to answer a question correctly is the winner, and receives some cherry pie.

7. *Colonial Party*

Students may dress up in colonial costume. Each table of the library media center displays books and book lists, exhibits, and dioramas on a topic. Cooking in colonial America—the materials, the food, some recipes, and actual samples to taste—can be exhibited at one table. Other exhibits may include health and medicine in colonial times; Christmas and other holidays; stores and markets; schools; loggers and sawmills; travel in colonial times; artisans; city life; farm life; pastime activities; storybooks; home life; settler children; village life; etc. Create an exhibit of conveniences unknown in those days: electric stoves, typewriters, vacuum cleaners, telephones, electric lights, trains, cars, airplanes, refrigerators, etc. The history class will particularly enjoy this "party," although some of the other subject teachers may like to drop by with their classes to see what's going on.

8. *Hobby Show*

Invite students to bring their hobbies into the library media center to share with the other students: airplane models, collections of baseball cards, stamp or coin collections, art, needlecrafts, small woodwork, or whatever. Students may speak on their hobbies to small groups, explaining how they got interested in their hobbies and how they pursue them.

9. Hobby Workshop

The library media center may sponsor a workshop after school for students who are interested in finding out about a hobby. Invite other teachers, outside sources, and students to show other students how to maintain the hobby.

10. St. Patrick's Party

Students may make shamrock invitations to this party, and they may be placed in the teachers' mailboxes, or hand-delivered. Decorate the library media center with shamrocks, green paper, daffodils and jonquils. This party may concentrate on "green" and Irish themes which can be correlated to all or most of the subjects of the curriculum.

The geography of Ireland may be displayed with an Irish map. The geography teacher may give an assignment on Ireland or the Irish culture and customs. English classes may compose limericks, or they may read some Irish folklore and short stories. The home economics class may make some "green" food. Students may guess at some Irish conundrums or riddles, with the winner getting a prize. The math class may find materials at one of the tables on banking and money. Science may find a table on plants and photosynthesis materials. The guidance table may provide books about the "green" emotion, jealousy.

11. April Fool's Festival

Around April 1, prepare for a day of foolery. Invite the science or math class to exhibit or perform optical illusions from books borrowed from the library. English classes may construct foolish rhymes, and the library media center may hold a foolish rhyming contest. Students may select books on humor to read and report on. Any student who laughs then must give a report on a humorous book. The art class may exhibit cartoons or caricatures of the teachers.

12. *Birthday Banquet*

Designate each of twelve tables in the media center to represent one month of the calendar year. Each table displays biographies of famous people born in that month, and books by authors born in that month. Include famous inventors with photocopied materials on their creations, and books appropriate for the topic.

13. *Seasonal Banquet*

Perk up the atmosphere, and hold a spring, summer, fall, or winter banquet in your library media center. Design bulletin board displays and activities, projects and exhibits, and bibliographies and book displays to correspond to the season and the activity. To liven up the school during the January winter doldrums, for example, show a video on the basic techniques of skiing. Invite a ski instructor to make a short visit to the school to give a couple of tips on skiing. Sell tickets to the nearby ski lodge for an after-school ski trip, or tickets to an ice skating rink. A faculty member may be in charge of the ski club. Serve hot cocoa. Display all kinds of books on hobbies one can do indoors during the stormy weather. So much can be done with a little imagination.

14. *Baby Contest*

One student from each of the homerooms may bring in his or her baby picture to display in the library. Students may guess to whom the pictures belong, and the student who guesses the most wins a prize. Clues may be written under the pictures.

15. *Carnation Day*

On this day students may come to the library to purchase a carnation for $1. An adult library aide or volunteer may help with this endeavor. Carnation Day may also be dress-up day for the students. Carnations may be procured from the local grocery store florist.

16. Valentine's Day

Any student coming to the library media center on this day may receive candy hearts. Award roses to five students entering the center at intervals that have been secretly predetermined: for example, the seventh, ninth, twenty-fourth, thirty-second, and fiftieth students to enter the center that day.

17. Newbery Author Invitation

Invite a Newbery Award–winning author to the library to speak to various English classes. Write to the publisher of the book to obtain the author's address, or send the letter directly to the publisher. Also, the Society of Children's Book Writers has a roster that includes writers who are members of SCBW and their addresses. You must join the society to obtain the roster, and this might be expensive, but what if you have some kind of fundraiser to earn the money? Having an author speak would really boost interest in books.

18. Local Author

Perhaps there is an author who resides locally. Someone may have been written up in the newspaper, and may not be nationally famous, but may have published a book. Invite that author to the library for a visit.

19. Overdue Pizza Party

The five students who have the least number of overdue books taken out of the school library at the end of a marking period will win a pizza party.

20. Mystery Book

Students may visit the library media center to guess the title of a well-known fiction book. Clues will be located on the bulletin board and around the library. The winning student will receive a delectable prize.

21. *Library Give-Out Day*

Pick a day when every student who comes to the library media center receives some small token: a pencil, a sticker, a candy bar, whatever.

22. *Library Mystery Day*

Pick a day to give a prize to the student who enters the library on a "lucky number" that has been secretly predetermined: the fifth student to enter, or the twenty-fifth, or whatever. The surprise could be a pocket dictionary or a popular magazine.

23. *Sequestered Secrets*

Type up a secret code and post it on the library media center bulletin board. Students must visit the media center in order to decipher the message. The code could be socially geared, in that it gives information about various students or teachers, something that students would not tire of, and would desire to find out. The message should be innocuous—for example, a message about how members of the baseball team played, and what happened at the game; or some interesting tidbit regarding a teacher.

24. *Sports Hero*

Invite a local sports figure from the town, a popular and well-known college sports hero, or a professional sports figure to speak to the student body about playing a sport. The sports person could speak in the library to various groups of students. We had twin-sister Olympic swimming champions living in the town come to visit our school.

25. Position Available

At the beginning of the school year, post help-wanted dittos around the school in order to advertise openings available for library aide positions. Write a brief job description, and instructions on how to apply for becoming a library aide. Include any deadlines. Have an announcement of the "position available" made over the school radio system.

26. Library Aides Award Party

Hold a celebration for the library aides at the end of the year, or at the end of each trimester if the school is a middle school. Students will receive awards for being helpful in the library. All the aides should be given some type of award. Aides may receive awards for showing the most interest in doing library work; being the most courteous at all times; being neat; being dependable; never missing their library aide times.

Cake, punch, potato chips, or any other party food may be brought into the library by the librarian and the aides. Awards may be anything from food certificates to posters or anything of interest to the students.

27. Book Take-Out

The student who has checked out the most books during a marking period or trimester may be awarded a prize. Gift certificates or a pizza party may be the prize.

28. Library Media Center Faculty Quiz

Prepare a humorous questionnaire for the faculty. Ask them to return completed quizzes to the library. The quizzes will call their attention to the library, and the answers will give helpful insights to both faculty and librarians.

Name_____ **Grade / Subject**_____ **Score**____

1. The last time I was in the library media center was

____can't remember (– 50 points)
____I think last year, or the year before (1 point)
____last week (4 points)
____yesterday (5 points)
____today (10 points)

2. The last time I used the public library was

____when I was in high school or college (– 5 points)
____this year (20 points)
____I don't know, but at least I have a valid library card (10 points)
____before my library card expired (2 points)
____I have no idea where the public library is (– 30 points)

3. How often do you give the library media specialist advance notice of assignments?

____I always inform the library media specialist (10 points)
____I usually inform (5 points)
____sometimes (2 points)
____never (– 5 points)

4. I preview audiovisuals before using them in the class:

____always (7 points) *Don't lie!*
____sometimes (4 points)
____never (1 point) *At least you're honest!*

5. I suggest books and audiovisual materials to the library media specialist that would be beneficial to class teaching:

____each year (10 points)
____each fall (5 points)
____whenever I'm asked (10 points)
____continuously (10 points)
____why bother (0 points)

6. I send individual students, small groups, and bring my class to the library media center

_____regularly (20 points)
_____occasionally (10 points)
_____not very often, 2 or 3 times a year (1 point)
_____never (– 20 points)

7. How comfortable do you feel about using the library media center, the card catalog, locating books and reference books, etc.?

_____I know it like the back of my hand (30 points)
_____fairly comfortable (20 points)
_____comfortable in some sections, but not in others (10 points)
_____I don't know where to begin to look (– 10 points)

8. When you need audiovisual equipment, how much time do you give notice?

_____1 week (10 points)
_____3 days (5 points)
_____1 day (2 points)
_____30 minutes (1 point)
_____none, I just want the equipment when I ask (– 5 points)

9. When was the last time that you used the library for recreational reading?

_____this week (10 points)
_____this school year (3 points)
_____last year (1 point)
_____I only read in bed at night (– 5 points)

10. The last time I used media either borrowed from or produced by the library media center was

_____before Edison's inventions, I used cartoons (– 10 points)
_____last year (– 5 points)
_____this year (5 points)
_____last class period (10 points)

Scoring:
80 and above—You're terrific!!
40–80—Not bad; you're acceptable!!
20–40—You're a little shaky!
Below 20—You're completely lost!!! We've got a Media Map for you!

29. *Parent Conference Night*

During the evenings or afternoons when parent conferences are scheduled with the teachers, the library media center is usually passed right by unless you cause it to get some attention. Make up some publicity posters, and place them in several corridors of the school. Do not forget to hang one in the main entrance of the school. Parents will not be able to miss them as they wander around and wait to speak to teachers, and you have called attention to the library, even if not all parents come by. They just might stop by to see what all the fuss is about, especially if you create brightly colored and exciting posters.

Design an eye-catching entrance display outside the library door. A blinking light or sign would certainly cause attention. Inside the media center, create vivid and exciting displays of books, student projects, and activities on the tables and counters. Photocopy a one-page summary of recent library activity and the school's library media center program for parents to take home with them. Parents may not be aware of how active the media center can be, and may be pleasantly surprised; they may encourage their children to use the library even more.

30. *On the Air*

Call the local radio or TV station, and try selling them on interviewing you about the activities going on in the library media center.

31. *Write a Booklet*

Put together a booklet describing the library media center's program. This could be quite impressive to the superintendent of schools, the board of education, and school administrators.

32. Principal's Message

If the principal of your school usually sends home to the parents an occasional message about the school's happenings and activities of interest, write up one segment about the library media center, and give it to the principal to include in his or her message. When the principal includes such news in a message home, parents will get the impression that the library media center is considered an important place.

33. Newspaper Interview

Contact a news reporter for the local newspaper, and tell him or her what an exciting and active place the library media center is. Tell briefly about the entire year's schedule, and what makes the library media center so special and meaningful to the students. Invite the reporter to visit the library during a specific activity to take a photograph of the event and include it in the newspaper. The more publicity, the more students and teachers will come to know the library as a comfortable and interesting place.

34. Faculty Notices

Send occasional news releases to the faculty of the school, enlightening them on recent programs and activities, displays, bibliographies, taped TV specials, anything that may lure them into the library. Remember that teachers are usually afraid that changing the way they teach their classes will demand more time, which they simply do not have. Try to make them aware of how the library can fill one of their needs and *save* them some time.

35. News Releases

Post outside or inside the library photocopies of magazine and newspaper articles of topical interest. Or place articles of specific interest in a particular teacher's mailbox. For example, send articles about the greenhouse effect in our atmosphere to a science teacher or any other teacher that has expressed an interest in it. (One teacher asked me for articles on apples and daminozide, since she was concerned about giving unsafe apple juice to her toddler.) The teachers will become aware of how much information the library can provide on special topics of interest to them or their classes.

36. Rationale

Send the board of education and the superintendent of schools a one-page summary explaining the year's library media center programs. Let them know that the library is an active place. Also explain specifically how the library supports the curriculum, and emphasize that with greater funds the library could do much more. Write up a second page, a budget rationale. Indicate how many volumes are held — an inventory count of science, math, history, classics, etc. — and cite the approximate copyright dates to indicate those that are out of date. Compare your inventory figures with the state's standard for number of volumes per number of students. Give them facts and figures. Show them what the library could be with proper funds.

37. Student Guide

Design a student guide to help students become oriented to the library at the beginning of the school year. Besides a map, the guide may contain examples of how and where to find specific information in the card catalog, general and specific reference books, and the *Readers' Guide*.

38. Library Fundraiser

Hold a fundraiser at any time of the school year to collect funds for books, special collections, or simply for prizes and materials used in the media center activities. The bake sale is an old standby, or try a book fair, ticket sales to a dance or some school event, or a raffle for posters. The fundraiser itself creates excitement, something different, and a reason to go to the library.

39. Library Newsletter

Create a newsletter, and send it to parents, faculty, and administrators. Outline the library media center's program as was done for Parent Conference Night (page 11).

40. Videotape

Tape an interview with students, a short play, or other library media center activities, and run the tape continuously for a day or two in one corner of the library. Students will flock into the library to view themselves and their friends.

41. Quiet Reading Time

The library media center may sponsor a quiet reading time each day (or once a week) in cooperation with the principal. For a 30 to 60 minute period during the school day, every student must have a book, either from his own collection or from the library, and is to read silently during this time.

42. Special Library Night

Invite parents to the library media center (similar to Parent Conference Night, page 11) for a special library evening. Have a running videotape on library activities; displays on student projects; catchy book displays; bibliographies on family life, family problems and bibliotherapy type of resources for browsing; examples of media production such as filmstrips or videos that were produced by the library; lists of vacation or sick day reading; reviews of books and encyclopedias; etc. Serve coffee and tea and cookies. The volunteer workers and the library aides club may help show the library to the parents.

43. Library Meeting Place

If space and scheduling allow, you may invite one or two of the faculty to hold a parent conference in the library media center. This may call attention to the importance of the media center. In the conference, the teacher, psychologist, or guidance counselor could use media (videocassettes, slides, etc.) that were produced in conjunction with the library.

44. Media Workshop

Offer to hold a media production workshop for the teachers. Discuss transparencies, films, filmstrips with audio, photography, still pictures, graphic materials, etc.

45. Hobby Addresses

Students pursuing a hobby may locate addresses for supplies and equipment from the library media center. Publicize an address or two on a poster, and indicate that whatever the hobby, there are catalogs available if they write requesting them.

46. Bibliography Lists

We have compiled many fiction lists, and make them available to students and teachers: mysteries, classics, contemporary classics, futuristic novels, etc. Students can use these lists to proceed directly to the fiction section in order to select a book, especially if there is a crowd at the card catalog. Post the lists, and give them to teachers.

47. Library Month

In April, celebrate library month or library week with a daily or weekly event. Make some waves, make some noise, cause a mild stir at that time. Do something to get attention for the library, and make it inviting for students. Do something to make them want to come to the center.

48. *Student Questionnaire*

Prepare a student questionnaire to find out about student body attitude toward the library media center. Use this in promoting good library attitudes. For example:

1. I am in the   ____seventh grade   ____eighth grade.
2. I come to the library media center   ____daily   ____weekly ____occasionally   ____never.
3. I mainly come to the library media center to   ____read ____do homework   ____research   ____relax.
4. I come to the library media center mainly for ____academic reasons   ____social reasons.
5. The library media center atmosphere is   ____noisy ____just right   ____too quiet.
6. I use the public library   ____often   ____sometimes ____never.
7. The three things I most like about the library media center are:

   _____

   _____

   _____

8. The three things I most dislike about the library media center are:

   _____

   _____

   _____

9. How has the library media center helped you most so far?

   _____ .

10. How helpful has your library research skills class (if you have been in one) been?   ____not at all   ____somewhat ____extremely.
11. Library media centers are   ____OK   ____too easy ____too demanding in dealing with students.
12. What changes would you make in the library media center program, if any, and why? _____

   _____ .

13. How often do you use the following items? Answer "O" for often, "S" for seldom, "N" for never.

____fiction books   ____vertical file

____nonfiction books   ____xerox machine

____magazines   ____audiovisual equipment

____special reference books   ____records

____general reference books   ____multimedia kits

____reserve materials   ____cassettes

14. Students should be able to do the following in the library media center: ____meet with friends ____eat ____speak freely.

15. The library media specialist and staff are ____extremely helpful ____somewhat helpful ____very seldom helpful.

49. *Dirty Drugs Month*

Compile and display lists of books on drugs, both fiction and nonfiction. Invite a speaker from the local hospital to talk about the effects of drugs on the body. Display visuals of the bad effects of drugs throughout the school and library.

50. *Balloon Delivery*

Write up short announcements inviting classes to some grand event about to take place in the library. Slip them inside balloons before inflating, or clip them to the strings on already-inflated balloons. Have a library aide deliver the balloons to the classes.

51. *Unreasonable Excuses*

Display a list of excuses of why a book is late being returned to the library media center. The most original and ingenious excuse wins a prize.

52. Book Delinquents

Post outside the library a list of students who have overdue books. These are the students who must return all books before taking out any more, or attending school functions, etc.

53. Book Appreciation Day

Sponsor a book appreciation day. Prepare an exhibit showing how books are made, the history of books, how to care for books, book publishing, and any related topics.

54. VIP Award

A student who has read every book on a particular list (such as a Newbery Award Fiction Book list) may be cited for the "VIP Award." This student should get special recognition as well as special treatment for the day. Perhaps another student can carry the VIP's books around all day, or the VIP may have special locker and lavatory privileges for the school day. A plaque can be awarded to the student. The student will have written a summary or a book report on each book proving it was indeed read.

55. Birthday Boy or Girl

A student may have his or her birthday announced by the office, and the student may then come to the library to pick up a surprise. Students may receive bookmarks, candy bars, or anything that would be a good birthday surprise.

56. Care Packages

The library media specialist may prepare a school vacation, rainy day, or sick day "care package" for students. Various packages may include 2 or 3 books, plus a bibliography of other interesting books to read.

57. *Most Books Read Award*

Give an award for the most books read during a month or during a marking period.

58. *Classic Jigsaw*

Design a jigsaw puzzle for some of the classic fiction books. Make some photocopies of the book jacket with title blacked out, plus the first page or a famous page from the book. Students must put the puzzle together, and decide the name of the book. This activity may be used as a contest or as an individual activity.

59. *School Newspaper*

Give the school newspaper editors some exciting news bulletin about upcoming events in the media center; also publicize past events. Blow your horn as much and as loudly as possible to bring the library to the attention of everyone.

60. *Fortune-Cookie Take-Out*

The home economics class may whip up some Chinese fortune cookies or some other goody for the student body to buy. Take-out may be located in the media center. Cookies may be placed in small lunch bags, and "fortunes" or messages may be placed inside. Watch the students gobble them down.

61. *Wonderful Wednesdays*

Have a day where all overdue books may be returned to the library media center without the usual fines being paid. Create a party atmosphere with streamers and balloons.

62. *Illustrator's Day*

Illustrators of published books, either fiction or nonfiction, may visit the school library media center. They can speak to students about how they got started in their careers, and what the editors are looking for when choosing an illustrator for a book.

63. *Author's Birthday*

Celebrate a local or famous author's birthday by inviting one to the school. Although this may be expensive, perhaps funds may be raised through various activities, and perhaps the schools in the district can help share the cost, especially if the author is shared. Display the books and advertise the upcoming event. Students can become excited about seeing a real famous author at their school and having a chance to ask questions.

64. *Potato Chip Raffle*

Hold a daily drawing from names of people who have checked out a book that day. The lucky winner receives a bag of potato chips or other sought-after goody.

65. *Black History Month*

Celebrate Black History Month in February by noting past and current accomplishments of black Americans. We have various large posters of famous black Americans displayed. Ask the Association for the Study of Afro-American Life and History (ASALH) what the theme is for that year.

Invite a local black leader of the NAACP to speak at the school library. Display and publish lists of books by and about black Americans.

66. *Rap Session*

Hold a weekly or bi-monthly rap session with students and a couple of faculty members participating. A committee of students and faculty may suggest topics.

67. *Costume Day*

Choose a day that everyone may dress up as a book character, a famous person in history or a current celebrity. Advertise this upcoming event. Each class or homeroom may parade through the library media center, and the library media specialist may choose a winner from the class. Each winning costume-wearer wins a prize and is announced at the end of the day.

68. *Book-Record-Cassette Swap*

In a corner of the library media center, set up book-record-cassette swap boxes where students may deposit books, etc., that they no longer need. For each item that they bring in, they may remove one from the swap box, or else they may simply donate if they wish.

69. *Science Quizathon*

Students may sign up to be on either of two teams who will compete toward winning a great prize. Questions being asked will be taken from the science curriculum, and many of these questions will have been research questions given to the classes by their teachers. Students may have already located the answers in the library media center. The winning team will be treated to a great party! The team who receives the most points is the winner.

70. *Checkers Tournament*

Hold a checkers or some other type of tournament in the library media center between the students and the teacher. Several boards could be set up as an extracurricular activity after school. Advertise over the school radio or in the school paper the winners of the event.

71. Special Reference Permission

Students who have never brought a book back late may be allowed a special overnight or weekend borrowing privilege for reference books or reserve books.

72. Missing Books List

Post a missing books list, and advertise a reward for returning them to the library media center. Watch these books suddenly reappear! Make the reward something valuable, that is, a fast-food gift certificate, a bag of popcorn or potato chips, a rock star or car poster, etc.

73. Threatening Warnings

What lies in store for people who damage library property or books? Have a contest to see who can write the most frightening threats. These warnings should be no longer than four lines, and may rhyme.

74. Ten Best Books

Post a list of Newbery Award–winning books, classic books, contemporary classic books, or whatever you choose. Set up a ballot box in the library media center. Students may vote for the ten best books on the list.

75. All-Day Readathon

Sponsor an all-day readathon in cooperation with the administration. Students must have one or more books to read. The homeroom who is still reading quietly at the end of this readathon will be given a special pizza party or some other recognition. Each member of the homeroom must be reading until the end of the readathon.

76. *Volunteer Readers*

Students may participate in this very worthwhile program of reading to blind or visually impaired individuals, shut-ins, or people in nursing homes. Any student who has read for a minimum of ten hours may receive remuneration for his time.

77. *Endangered Species Week*

The library media center may sponsor an "Endangered Species Week." Display photos (color if possible) of animals on this list. Bring in a speaker from a nearby zoo or college to talk about the problems of these species. Offer to show videotapes of National Geographic specials to classes. Perhaps you may be able to invite a "traveling zoo" to come to the school to show a few of the animals.

78. *Monthly Party*

Celebrate each month with a party. Decorate the library media center with the appropriate touches. For the month of September, for example, put colored leaves on the bulletin boards and around the room, along with photographs of fall and late summer. Display books about fall sports such as football and soccer, and fiction titles on school stories and friendships. Prepare appropriate bibliographies of these titles to make available for students. The party may last 2 or 3 days to allow all students a chance to attend. Punch may be served. A "door prize" can be awarded to one of the students who attended the party.

79. *Country Fair*

Hold a "fair" in the library media center. Students may help prepare for the fair by preparing invitations, bringing in or arranging for other students to bring in exhibits, etc. Form a committee of students to help with this event.

The fair may consist of several tables or "booths" in the library. Exhibits of handicrafts may be displayed along with appropriate books (on airplane models, sewing, needlework, stamps, coins, dolls, etc.). A baby show consisting of baby pictures of teachers may be displayed along with an entry form for guessing the identities of the babies. A slide show of art exhibits from the art class may be included along with books on art. A stage show with a videotape of the English class performing a play or some other activity may be utilized. "Barkers" holding signs rather than shouting or announcing exhibits may be employed. Many curriculum subjects may be related and included.

80. Travelogue

Each member of the class will select a passport to a specific country from a box. They will then select one fiction book with the setting in the country chosen. Also, students will research the country in *Lands and People* (Grolier).

81. Who or What

Any subject class may participate in this activity. The history class, for example, may come to the library media center. Posted on the bulletin board are photos of presidents, famous statesmen, etc. Under the photos should be captions giving pertinent clues. Students will identify them.

82. Country Jigsaw

Laminate and back a map of a country and cut it into puzzle pieces. The geography class may participate in this project. Each person may piece together a separate puzzle of the country being studied. Whoever finishes his puzzle first wins.

83. *Storyteller's Convention*

Schedule a storyteller's convention. The library media specialist may present ten books to an English class in a booktalk fashion, and also use media such as tape recordings of the author reading his own book. If done well, students should want to borrow the books.

84. *World Jigsaw*

Laminate a world map, and back it with oak tag or other material. Cut it into pieces. The geography class may be divided into teams of three or four. The fastest team to piece together the puzzle should win a prize.

85. *A Historical Party*

Students may come to the library in historical garb representing a character in history. The library media specialist should dress up, too. Old historical photos and illustrations may decorate the room. Old songs may be sung; these may be borrowed from the music teacher or found in music books in the library. Students must tell something about themselves without disclosing their characters' names. The rest of the students must guess the characters that they are representing.

Students must, of course, first come to the library to get a biography or research reference materials about their character.

86. *Displays*

Locate an old mannequin from a junk shop or from a store, and dress it up according to the season or theme. We found a witch mannequin which is a wonderful addition to the Halloween season, or actually anytime of the year. We even dress her up at Christmas. Any outstanding display calls attention to the library media center.

87. Trivia Club

Form a trivia club. Students and the faculty advisors and the library media specialist may locate questions and answers in the library media center for a weekly meet. Any extracurricular club activity, such as the music or art club, may utilize the library media center for information.

88. Community Line

Whatever the activity, the library media center can provide clubs, groups, and other organizations, with information on concerts, exhibits, workshops, lectures, and special happenings around the community.

89. Library Line

The library media center may provide a line to the public library. Information on the public library's holdings, and a call to the public library requesting that it reserve books for a specific class, can be quite useful—especially if the school media center does not contain enough materials on a particular subject. Also, the state library may have regional centers with materials the school may borrow for use with the classes.

90. Book of the Week

Sponsor a book of the week by writing a short paragraph or two about a particular title. Try to write a "hook" that would interest students and spark their curiosity. This paragraph may be read over the school public address system, and also placed in the library media center window along with a copy of the book (when that goes, a copy of the book jacket).

91. *Did You Know?*

Send to the faculty a notice: "Did you know?" that the library media center has: various titles of magazines, reference books, various services available, etc.

92. *Teacher Award*

Give a certificate to the teacher who has made the most use of the library media center (combining class use and personal use). Announce the winner over the school public address system, and treat that teacher to lunch.

93. *Letters from Famous Authors*

The library media specialist and students may write letters to famous authors. Authors are especially nice people. I have always received a letter back, and some have been very personable and friendly. Post these responses on a bulletin board. Students are quite excited about the fact that you received a letter from Judy Blume!

94. *Cooperative Projects*

Students may be permitted to work cooperatively on projects in a special corner or area of the library media center as long as they do so without distracting the other students. The library media center can be a great place especially if you have areas built into the center that would accommodate such activity.

95. *Library Quiz*

Include this library quiz in the school newspaper or pass it out during orientation:

TRUE OR FALSE

1. All librarians wear glasses and wear their hair in tight buns. (False. Look at Ms. [Brown]!!)

2. Librarians enjoy saying "Quiet!" (False. They really get tired of having to shush people, but the library media center is for study and research, and sometimes students forget that.)

3. The library media center is a place for games and fun activities. (True! Teachers bring classes into the library media center for contests and learning games.)

4. The only way to find out if there is a particular book in the library media center is to ask the librarian. (False. Look at the subject cards in the card catalog.)

5. The only source of information in the library media center is books. (False. There are magazines, newspapers, the vertical file, maps, and audiovisual materials.)

6. The librarian gives out library passes in exchange for hot muffins made in the home economics class. (False. You must get a pass from your subject teacher.)

7. Books are arranged by the Library of Congress system of classification. (False. Dewey Decimal system of classification.)

8. To get the most current information on a topic, find a magazine article listed in one of the periodical indexes. (True. For example, the *Readers' Guide* and *National Geographic Index.)*

9. Fiction books are arranged by numbers, and nonfiction books are arranged by author. (False. It's the other way around. Fiction books are arranged alphabetically by author in a separate section; nonfiction books are arranged by number and initials of the author's name.)

10. The library media center is an "in" place to go where one can read for academics, vocationally, and recreationally. (True.)

96. *Halloween Haunting*

During the Halloween season, hang spiders and webs around the library media center, turn the lights off (if everyone can still see his or her way around), and turn the library media center into an eerie scene. Wear a witch's costume. Students will want to see the place out of curiosity.

97. *Media Club*

The media club may be trained in helping to produce some of the media, and in charge of delivering equipment to teachers. They also enjoy operating the equipment, and often are quicker in learning operation than the teachers. Helping with the media gives students a sense of importance.

98. *Library Button Day*

Whoever is not wearing a library media center button on this day gets an essay assignment or additional homework at the end of the day.

99. *Baseball Clinic*

Invite a local college baseball star or a high school coach to speak about techniques of the game. Students may sign up for the clinic in the library media center. A film may be shown at this clinic after school.

100. *Class Productions*

Invite the art, industrial arts, math or other department to exhibit class work in the library media center. Students' names may or may not be listed under their work. Students coming into the library media center may vote for the project that they think is the best.

101. December Gift Exchange

During the month of December, students may bring into the library media center an inexpensive, wrapped, grab-bag gift (set a price limit) and deposit it in the gift box. During the holiday week, any student who has brought in a gift may come to the library media center to select a gift from the box. Student names who have deposited may be typed into the computer, or kept on a list by the library assistant.

102. Library Slogan

Sponsor a contest for the best library slogan. The slogan should be a short catchy saying enticing students to utilize the library media center. The winner should receive a nice surprise.

103. Bookends Dance

Sponsor a dance. At least it will make the entire student body aware that the library media center is alive and well. Charge a nominal fee, $1–$2, for tickets. Proceeds may go toward that updated encyclopedia set or whatever is crucially needed in the library.

104. Topic Week

Feature a topic during any week of the year such as gun control, nuclear arms, skateboarding, karate—anything. Display fiction, non-fiction, magazine articles, vertical file material, and reference materials on the topic. Invite teachers to bring their classes into the library media center to read about and explore the topic.

105. Booking Professionals

Ask the faculty for suggestions, and try booking professionals for a special lecture, class or clinic at your school library media center. A simple phone call or letter is really all it takes, and it works wonders for public relations. For example, even a high school student who has gone on a trip abroad to study in a foreign language program may come to speak to the French or Spanish class, and tell of his or her experience in that country.

106. Homework Aid Clearinghouse

The library media center may serve as a clearinghouse for students who would like examples of good book reports, paragraphs, and other such writing. Students may look in a file. Student tutors may also be arranged, and students needing help could sign up in the library media center.

107. Best Homeroom

The homeroom with the fewest overdue books during a marking period should definitely win a pizza party or something special. This is a great way to help the overdue book problem.

108. Xerox Copier

Ever since we had a copying machine installed in the library media center, not only have theft and vandalism decreased, but students are using reference books even more since they are able to have the material copied.

109. On-Line

This one is a dream! We do not have it, of course, since it is much too expensive. Going on-line gives access to any book, document, or journal in the world. Perhaps a nearby large public, special or university library has on-line facilities that you might have access to if a faculty member is in desperate need.

110. Reference Week

Sponsor a reference week by making up 10 to 15 questions, and using them for a week-long contest. The winner will be the first student to answer all questions correctly (or to have the most correct answers). Students should write on their answer sheets the date and period on which they were completed. Display the reference books on the counter or in the hallway display window with a caption such as: "If you had used these references, you would have found the reference week answers."

111. Happygram

Write a brief note of praise home to parents commending their son or daughter for always bringing books back on time, or whatever positive behavior you can think of. Type a form letter for various categories of good behavior ahead of time, and then simply fill in the names.

112. You're on Camera

Videotape students as they come into the library media center, and replay the tape in a corner of the library. Watch students flock into the library media center!

113. Library Commercial

Write a 30 to 60 second library commercial, and read it or have it read over the school public address system. Use the commercial to advertise a special upcoming event or program in the library media center.

114. Study Skills Clinic

Hold a series of after-school clinics on how to be an A student. Study skills would cover attitude, positive thinking, reasons for studying, planning each day, the right setting, note-taking, reference books, writing a report, taking a test, feeling bogged down, keeping yourself in good shape, and learning by doing.

115. Book Count

Advertise a contest where students must guess how many books are housed in the school library media center. The student coming closest to the correct inventory count wins a desirable prize.

116. Library Posters

Place various posters around the school advertising ways that the library media center can be of use. Students can make them up with some guidance, since they love working on posters. Give out a present to each of the students who makes up a worthwhile poster.

117. Telephone an Author

Tape a telephone conversation with a famous author. Play it for the school in the library media center. Or with today's technology, you may be able to talk live with a hookup so that students may ask questions and take part in the conversation. Students will love this!

118. How-To Books

Students in the writing class or other class could write a how-to "book" on some topic—for example, how to make a dress or how to fix a flat tire. Students would research their topic in the library media center. These books would be displayed in the library media center.

119. Teacher Workshop

Hold a meeting at the beginning of the school year in order to orient the faculty as to the services that the library media center provides. Some of the things that the library can do for students and teachers include:

1. Library skills development using a variety of instructional materials and teaching strategies.
2. Reading guidance: help students develop a love and an appreciation of reading for informational, vocational, and recreational purposes.
3. Reference services.
4. Assistance to faculty in gathering materials for teaching lessons.
5. Compilation of bibliographies.
6. Dissemination of information on field trips, TV programs, and services of special interest.
7. AV equipment and materials.
8. Assistance to teachers in developing an activity in order to emphasize a point or lesson to be learned.
9. Gathering of materials for research on a project or to be put on reserve.
10. Design of individualized learning projects for remediation.
11. Gathering of materials to produce a lesson if the textbook is inadequate.
12. Assistance to teachers in designing, implementing, and evaluating instruction.

120. "Miss..."

This "beauty" contest may include boys dressed up as girls. Take photos of the contestants, and post them on the bulletin board in the library media center. Students may vote for the most gorgeous "Miss...."

121. Special Librarian

Become useful to the principal, board of education and superintendent. Serve them in any way possible by providing information and materials. Let them know you can be helpful with *their* needs.

122. *Bookmark Bazaar*

Students may compete in a bookmark contest, creating the most unique library bookmarks. Bookmark entries may be exhibited in the library media center, with the winner receiving a delightful surprise! The winning bookmark should be duplicated for library media center use.

123. *Field Trip*

Arrange for a field trip to the public library for the English class or other classes. Advertise that the public library's holdings can expand the school library collection.

124. *Library Media Center Raffle*

Hold a raffle where every student who enters the library media center has his or her name deposited into a box. At the end of the day, the library media specialist draws a name out of the box, and that person (with the permission of the principal) does not have to do any homework for that night.

II. FUN WITH BOOK LISTS

125. Metaphoric Madness

Locate as many fiction titles as you can with the words "as" or "like" in the title, or that contain a metaphor.

1. *Just Like Jenny.* (Asher)
2. *Otherwise Known as Sheila the Great.* (Blume)
3. *A Funny Girl Like Me.* (O'Donnell)
4. *The Heart Is a Lonely Hunter.* (McCullers)
5. *The One in the Middle Is the Green Kangaroo.* (Blume)
6. *Almost Like Sisters.* (Cavanna)
7. *A Shadow Like a Leopard.* (Levoy)
8. *You Are the Rain.* (Knudson)
9. *A Boy Like Walt.* (Clewes)
10. *My Darling, My Hamburger.* (Zindel)

126. Kissing Booth

Find as many titles as you can in the school library that have to do with going steady, kissing, and romance:

1. *Nancy and Nick.* (Cooney)
2. *Going Steady.* (Emery)
3. *Kisses for Sale.* (Enderle)
4. *Recipe for Romance.* (Field)
5. *Please Don't Kiss Me Now.* (Gerber)
6. *Dating Blues.* (Johnson)
7. *A Kiss for Tomorrow.* (Johnson)

8. *Once Upon a Kiss.* (Mendonca)
9. *Stolen Kisses.* (Reynolds)
10. *Supercouple.* (Towne)

127. Cascade of Waterfalls

Find titles that mention water, rain, or bodies of water.

1. *Cold River.* (Judson)
2. *The Sea Robbers.* (Kraske)
3. *River of Death.* (MacLean)
4. *The Rains Came.* (Bromfield)
5. *The Sea of Grass.* (Richter)
6. *Watership Down.* (Adams)
7. *The Castle in the Sea.* (O'Dell)
8. *You Are the Rain.* (Knudson)
9. *Dragons in the Water.* (L'Engle)
10. *Waterless Mountain.* (Armer)
11. *The Sea Wolf.* (London)
12. *Stream Runner.* (Seed)
13. *The Shining Pool.* (Carlson)
14. *The Rains of Eridan.* (Hoover)
15. *The Awakening Water.* (Kestevan)
16. *River of Gold.* (Cheshire)
17. *The Roaring River Mystery.* (Dixon)
18. *Dreamland Lake.* (Peck)
19. *White Water, Still Water.* (Bosworth)

128. Light to Dark

Find titles that mention light, dark, or shadows.

1. *Good-Bye My Shadow.* (Stolz)
2. *Who Rides in the Dark.* (Meader)
3. *Danger on Shadow Mountain.* (Rumsey)
4. *The Journey of the Shadow Bairns.* (Anderson)
5. *The Shadow Guests.* (Aiken)

6. *Kept in the Dark.* (Bawden)
7. *Los Alamos Light.* (Bograd)
8. *The Mystery of the Laughing Shadow.* (Arden)
9. *The Keeper of the Isis Light.* (Hughes)
10. *The Dark Is Rising.* (Cooper)

129. Islands of Good Reading

Look for fiction books with the word "island" in the title.

1. *The Island of Helos.* (Butterworth)
2. *Treasure Island.* (Stevenson)
3. *Indiana Jones and the Curse of Horror Island.* (Stine)
4. *Mysterious Island.* (Verne)
5. *Big Blue Island.* (Gage)
6. *Spice Island Mystery.* (Cavanna)
7. *High and Haunted Island.* (Chauncy)
8. *Philippine Islands Surrender.* (White)
9. *Island of the Blue Dolphins.* (O'Dell)
10. *The Island Keeper.* (Mazer)

130. Hidden Pleasures

Look for fiction books whose titles suggest hidden places (caves, tunnels, etc.).

1. *Indiana Jones and the Cult of the Mummy's Crypt.* (Stine)
2. *Cave of Danger.* (Walton)
3. *Tunnel in the Sky.* (Heinlein)
4. *The Tombs of Atuan.* (Le Guin)
5. *Annerton Pit.* (Dickinson)
6. *Caves of Fire and Ice.* (Murphy)
7. *The Tunnel.* (Williams)
8. *Secret of the Haunted Crags.* (Hunt)
9. *Mystery of the Indian Cave.* (Issler)
10. *Mystery in Hidden Hollow.* (Jane)

131. Strange Places

Find fiction titles that mention foreign places.

1. *The Count of Monte Cristo.* (Dumas)
2. *Prisoner of Pedro Cay.* (Butterworth)
3. *The Prince of Omeya.* (Fon Eisen)
4. *The Hoard of the Himalayas.* (Healey)
5. *Miss Pickerell Goes to the Arctic.* (MacGregor)
6. *The Sniper at Zimba.* (Butterworth)
7. *Home to Harlem.* (McKay)
8. *Appointment in Samarra.* (O'Hara)
9. *The Bridge of San Luis Rey.* (Wilder)
10. *Sea Star; Orphan of Chincoteague.* (Henry)
11. *Men of Athens.* (Coolidge)
12. *The Skies of Crete.* (Forman)
13. *Nantucket Summer.* (Green)
14. *The Lion of the Kalahari.* (Hobson)
15. *The Virginian.* (Wister)
16. *Signpost to Switzerland.* (Allan)
17. *Secret of the Andes.* (Clark)
18. *Guns at Quebec.* (Dwight)
19. *Trumpeter of Krakow.* (Kelly)
20. *A Boy of Old Prague.* (Ish-Kishor)
21. *Passenger to Frankfurt.* (Christie)

132. Criminal Justice

Look for fiction books whose titles suggest crime and punishment.

1. *Confessions of a Teenage Baboon.* (Zindel)
2. *Confession of a Storyteller.* (Colman)
3. *Can You Sue Your Parents for Malpractice?* (Danzinger)
4. *The Diamond Smugglers.* (Butterworth)
5. *The Sniper at Zimba.* (Butterworth)
6. *Prisoner of Pedro Cay.* (Butterworth)
7. *The Sea Robbers.* (Kraske)
8. *Sing a Song of Ambush.* (Peyton)

9. *Cannibal Adventure.* (Price)
10. *The Executioner's Song.* (Mailer)
11. *The Confessions of Nat Turner.* (Styron)
12. *The Caine Mutiny.* (Wouk)
13. *A Killing Season.* (Brenner)
14. *Nop's Trials.* (McCraig)
15. *The Killer Swan.* (Clifford)
16. *Killer Music.* (Eisenberg)
17. *A Spy in Old Detroit.* (Emery)
18. *The Prisoner of Zenda.* (Hope)
19. *Stamp Twice for Murder.* (Cavanna)
20. *Kidnapped.* (Stevenson)
21. *Does This School Have Capital Punishment?* (Hentoff)
22. *When Hitler Stole Pink Rabbit.* (Kerr)
23. *A Hanging at Tyburn.* (Cross)
24. *The Traitor Queen.* (Faulkner)
25. *The Executioner.* (Bennett)
26. *Easy to Kill.* (Christie)
27. *A Murder Is Announced.* (Christie)
28. *Murder with Mirrors.* (Christie)
29. *The Case of the Blackmail Boys.* (Dicks)
30. *The Carnival Kidnap Caper.* (Dodson)

133. Dear . . .

Look for fiction titles containing "Miss," "Mrs.," "Ms.," or "Mr."

1. *Mrs. Mike.* (Freedman)
2. *Miss Pickerell Goes to the Arctic.* (MacGregor)
3. *Killing Mr. Griffin.* (Duncan)
4. *From the Mixed-Up Files of Mrs. Basil E. Frankweiler.* (Konigsburg)
5. *Miss Hickory.* (Bailey)
6. *Mrs. Frisby and the Rats of NIMH.* (O'Brien)
7. *Go Tell It to Mrs. Golightly.* (Cookson)
8. *Miss Lonelyhearts.* (West)
9. *Goodbye Mr. Chips.* (Hilton)
10. *What Mrs. McGillicuddy Saw.* (Christie)

134. *Sporting Diversions*

Find fiction titles that mention sports.

1. *Hang Glider.* (Bamman)
2. *Test Pilot.* (Bamman)
3. *Riffles for Watie.* (Keith)
4. *Racing in Her Blood.* (Altman)
5. *Grand Prix United States.* (Ashford)
6. *Dave White and the Electric Wonder Car.* (Butterworth)
7. *Marty and the Micro-Midgets.* (Butterworth)
8. *Road Racer.* (Butterworth)
9. *The Hockey Girls.* (Corbett)
10. *Skateboard Four.* (Bunting)
11. *Motorcycle Racer.* (Covington)
12. *Drag Race Driver.* (Douglas)
13. *Quarterback Walk-On.* (Dygard)
14. *Drag Strip.* (Gault)
15. *Wheels of Fortune.* (Gault)
16. *Dive from the Sky.* (Halacy)
17. *The Day of the Drag Race.* (Harkins)
18. *The Karate Kid.* (Hiller)
19. *Dive to Danger.* (Holmvik)
20. *Fury on Skates.* (Honig)
21. *Up Sails.* (Neigoff)
22. *Tennis Bum.* (Ogan)
23. *Drag Strip Challenge.* (Radlauer)
24. *Karting Challenge.* (Radlauer)
25. *Ollie's Team and the Baseball Computer.* (Philbrook)

135. *Hot-Cold*

Look for fiction books whose titles make you think of hot and cold.

1. *Big Man and the Burn-Out.* (Bess)
2. *Hell's Kitchen.* (Appel)
3. *London Snow: A Christmas Story.* (Theroux)

4. *Dive for the Sun.* (Love)
5. *On Firm Ice.* (Wilson)
6. *The Diary of Trilby Frost.* (Glaser)
7. *Caves of Fire and Ice.* (Murphy)
8. *The Nearest Fire.* (Wilder)
9. *Terror on the Ice.* (Neigoff)
10. *Blizzard.* (Curtis)

136. Castles in the Air

Look for fiction titles containing the word "castle."

1. *The Castle in the Sea.* (O'Dell)
2. *Mooncoin Castle; or Skulduggery Rewarded.* (Turkle)
3. *The Castle of Hape.* (Murphy)
4. *Castle in the Air.* (Westlake)
5. *The Secret of Castle Balou.* (Howe)
6. *We Have Always Lived in the Castle.* (Jackson)
7. *Castle.* (Macaulay)

137. Secrets

Find fiction books with secrets in the title.

1. *Secrets of the Shopping Mall.* (Peck)
2. *Secret Love.* (Steiner)
3. *Secret Places.* (Sallis)
4. *Secret of the Samurai Sword.* (Whitney)
5. *The Secret of the Missing Boat.* (Berna)
6. *Secret of the Indian Mound.* (Gage)
7. *The Secret of Castle Balou.* (Howe)
8. *Secret of the Haunted Crags.* (Hunt)
9. *The Secret of the Minstrel's Guitar.* (Keene)
10. *The Secret of Belledonne Room 16.* (Vries)
11. *Secret of the Stone Face.* (Whitney)
12. *The Secret of Stone House Farm.* (Young)

138. *Musically Inclined*

Look for fiction books whose titles mention music or musical instruments.

1. *Killer Music.* (Eisenberg)
2. *The Floating Opera.* (Barth)
3. *Don't Blame the Music.* (Cooney)
4. *Keep Stompin' Till the Music Stops.* (Pevsner)
5. *Sing a Song of Ambush.* (Peyton)
6. *Who Wants Music on Monday?* (Stolz)
7. *Drums Along the Mohawk.* (Edmonds)
8. *The Trumpeter of Krakow.* (Kelly)
9. *A Christmas Carol.* (Dickens)

139. *White Frost*

Find as many fiction titles as you can that contain the word "white."

1. *White Water, Still Water.* (Bosworth)
2. *Winter of the White Seal.* (Herbert)
3. *White Fang.* (London)
4. *Mercy Short: A Winter Journal, North Boston 1692–93.* (Farber)
5. *The White Twilight.* (Polland)
6. *White Stag.* (Seredy)
7. *Dave White and the Electric Wonder Car.* (Butterworth)
8. *Watch for a Tall White Sail.* (Bell)
9. *White Bird.* (Bulla)
10. *Flight of the White Wolf.* (Ellis)
11. *The Diary of Trilby Frost.* (Glaser)
12. *London Snow: A Christmas Story.* (Theroux)
13. *The Pearl.* (Steinbeck)

140. *Family Fiction*

Find fiction titles in the card catalog that include sons, daughters, fathers, and mothers.

1. *Cat-Man's Daughter.* (Abercrombie)
2. *Father Figure.* (Peck)
3. *Almost Like Sisters.* (Cavanna)
4. *My Brother Stevie.* (Clymer)
5. *The Truth About Fathers: A Novel.* (Gray)
6. *Denison's Daughter.* (Hall)
7. *Sweet Whispers, Brother Rush.* (Hamilton)
8. *Father's Arcane Daughter.* (Konigsburg)
9. *Three Sisters.* (Mazer)
10. *Baby Sister.* (Sachs)
11. *The Tynedale Daughters.* (Clark)
12. *My Father, the Coach.* (Slote)
13. *Blood Brother.* (Ruffell)
14. *My Brother Sam Is Dead.* (Collier)
15. *A Father Every Few Years.* (Bach)
16. *The Soul Brothers and Sister Lou.* (Hunter)

141. *Fictional Heights*

Find as many fiction titles as you can that include the word "mountain."

1. *Escape to Witch Mountain.* (Key)
2. *Return from Witch Mountain.* (Key)
3. *The Haunted Mountain.* (Hunter)
4. *The Mountain of Truth.* (Carlson)
5. *Waterless Mountain.* (Armer)
6. *The Hoard of the Himalayas.* (Healey)
7. *Danger on Shadow Mountain.* (Rumsey)
8. *The Dog that Watched the Mountain.* (Price)

142. Ghosts and Goblins

Locate as many fiction titles as you can that contain the word "ghost" or "goblin."

1. *Ghost Vision.* (Kortum)
2. *The Goblin Reservation.* (Simak)
3. *The Discontented Ghost.* (Corbett)
4. *What Beckoning Ghost.* (Lillington)
5. *The Ghost of Thomas Kempe.* (Lively)
6. *The Ghost Belonged to Me.* (Peck)
7. *Ghosts I Have Been.* (Peck)
8. *The Slavery Ghosts.* (Wallin)
9. *The Ghost of Ballyhooly.* (Cavanna)
10. *Ghost Lane.* (Curry)
11. *The Phantom of Walkaway Hill.* (Fenton)
12. *The Ghost of Five Owl Farm.* (Gage)
13. *The Ghost on the Hill.* (Gordon)
14. *The Mystery of the Crimson Ghost.* (Whitney)
15. *Ghost Dog of Killicut.* (Ellis)

143. Fiction: States

In the card catalog, locate fiction titles that are about states in the United States. They do not have to contain the state's name in the title.

1. *Two Sieges of the Alamo.* (Alter) Putman, 1965. (Texas)
2. *Waterless Mountain.* (Armer) McKay, 1959. (Arizona)
3. *Wilderness Teacher.* (Ball) Rand McNally, 1956. (Florida)
4. *The Wonderful Year.* (Barnes) Messner, 1946. (Colorado)
5. *Watch for a Tall White Sail.* (Bell) Morrow, 1948. (Alaska)
6. *A Gathering of Days; A New England Girl's Journal, 1830–32; A Novel.* (Blos) Scribner, 1979. (New Hampshire)
7. *Los Alamos Light.* (Bograd) Farrar, 1983. (New Mexico)
8. *The Search of Mary Katherine Mulloy.* (Bolton) Nelson, 1974. (California)
9. *Waikiki Beachboy.* (Brennan) Chilton, 1962. (Hawaii)
10. *White Bird.* (Bulla) Crowell, 1966. (Tennessee)
11. *Queenie Peavy.* (Burch) Viking, 1966. (Georgia)
12. *Skinny.* (Burch) Viking, 1964. (Georgia)

13. *The Hour of the Wolf.* (Calvert) New American Library, 1983. (Alaska)
14. *A Spell Is Cast.* (Cameron) Little, 1964. (California)
15. *Winter of the Whale.* (Carse) Putnam, 1961. (Long Island)
16. *Ski Racer.* (Casewit) Four Winds, 1968. (Colorado)
17. *Growin' Pains.* (Christian) Viking Penguin, 1987. (Texas)
18. *Paco's Miracle.* (Clark) Farrar, Straus, 1962. (New Mexico)
19. *The Luckiest Girl.* (Cleary) Morrow, 1958. (California)
20. *Minutemen of the Sea.* (Cluff) Follett, 1955. (Maine)
21. *The Enchanted; An Incredible Tale.* (Coatsworth) Pantheon, 1968. (Maine)
22. *The Last of the Mohicans.* (Cooper) Danbury Press, 1973. (New York)
23. *We Were There at the Battle of the Alamo.* (Cousins) Grosset & Dunlap, 1958. (Texas)
24. *Blizzard.* (Curtis) Dutton, 1970. (Idaho)
25. *Deliverance.* (Dickey) Dell, 1971. (Georgia)
26. *No Moon on Graveyard Head.* (Dorian) McGraw, 1953. (Maine)
27. *Wilderness Peril.* (Dygard) Morrow, 1985. (Minnesota)
28. *Drums Along the Mohawk.* (Edmonds) Bantam, 1950. (New York)
29. *The Matchlock Gun.* (Edmonds) Dodd, Mead, 1941. (New York)
30. *Flight of the White Wolf.* (Ellis) Holt, Rinehart & Winston, 1970. (Wisconsin)
31. *Ghost Dog of Killicut.* (Ellis) Four Winds Press, 1969. (Michigan)
32. *Hurry-Up Harry Hanson.* (Ellis) Four Winds Press, 1972. (Wisconsin)
33. *Thimble Summer.* (Enright) Hold, 1938. (Wisconsin)
34. *The Wind Blows Free.* (Erdman) Dodd, Mead, 1952. (Texas)
35. *The Immigrants.* (Fast) Dell, 1977. (California)
36. *Second Son.* (Faulkner) Colonial Williamsburg, 1969. (Virginia)
37. *Cimarron.* (Ferber) Grosset & Dunlap, 1930. (Oklahoma)
38. *Five Complete Novels.* (Ferber) Avenel, 1981. (Oklahoma)
39. *Calico Bush.* (Field) Macmillan, 1966. (Maine)
40. *Me and My Little Brain.* (Fitzgerald) Dial, 1971. (Utah)

41. *Brady*. (Fritz) Coward-McCann, 1960. (Pennsylvania)
42. *A Gathering of Old Men*. (Gaines) Knopf, 1983. (Louisiana)
43. *Fours Crossing*. (Garden) Scholastic, 1981. (New Hampshire)
44. *Blue Willow*. (Gates) Viking, 1968. (California)
45. *Old Yeller*. (Gipson) Harper & Row, 1956. (Texas)
46. *Foxy*. (Griffith) Greenwillow, 1984. (Florida)
47. *Uphill All the Way*. (Hall) Scribner, 1984. (Oklahoma)
48. *Sky Carnival; A Story of the Barnstorming Days*. (Hallstead) McKay, 1969. (Texas)
49. *The House of Dies Drear*. (Hamilton) Macmillan, 1968. (Ohio)
50. *Look for the Stars*. (Hill) Berkley, 1967. (Wisconsin)
51. *The Mystery of Dolphin Inlet*. (Holding) Macmillan, 1968. (Florida)
52. *The Legend of Sleepy Hollow*. (Irving) Watts, 1966. (New York)
53. *Rip Van Winkle & the Legend of Sleepy Hollow*. (Irving) Macmillan, 1963. (New York)
54. *Ramona*. (Jackson) Little, Brown, 1939. (California)
55. *...Sod-House Winter*. (Judson) Follett, 1957. (Minnesota)
56. *Smugglers' Island*. (King) Washburn, 1970. (South Carolina)
57. *...And Now Miguel*. (Krumgold) Crowell, 1953. (New Mexico)
58. *Strawberry Girl*. (Lenski) Dell, 1967. (Florida)
59. *Call of the Wild & Other Stories*. (London) Dodd, Mead & Co., 1960. (Alaska)
60. *White Fang*. (London) Macmillan, 1934. (Alaska)
61. *Betsy and Joe*. (Lovelace) Crowell, 1948. (Minnesota)
62. *Betsy in Spite of Herself*. (Lovelace) Crowell, 1946. (Minnesota)
63. *Betsy Was a Junior*. (Lovelace) Crowell, 1947. (Minnesota)
64. *Betsy's Wedding*. (Lovelace) Crowell, 1955. (Minnesota)
65. *Heaven to Betsy*. (Lovelace) Crowell, 1945. (Minnesota)
66. *Moccasin Trail*. (McGraw) Coward-McCann, 1952. (Oregon)
67. *Dance with Me*. (Madison) Scholastic, 1981. (California)
68. *Everglades Adventure*. (Meader) Harcourt, Brace & World, 1957. (Florida)
69. *Who Rides in the Dark?* (Meader) Harcourt, 1937. (New Hampshire)

70. *Big Doc's Girl.* (Medearis) Pyramid, 1950. (Arkansas)
71. *Centennial.* (Michener) Fawcett, 1974. (Colorado)
72. *Hawaii.* (Michener) Fawcett, 1959. (Hawaii)
73. *Kite.* (Minus) Viking, 1985. (South Carolina)
74. *Gentle Ben.* (Morey) Avon, 1976. (Alaska)
75. *Montana.* (O'Connor) Criterion, 1970. (Montana)
76. *Alexandra.* (O'Dell) Fawcett Juniper, 1984. (Florida)
77. *My Friend Flicka.* (O'Hara) Lippincott, 1941. (Wyoming)
78. *Best Wishes, Joe Brady.* (Osborne) Dial, 1984. (North Carolina)
79. *Love Always, Blue.* (Osborne) Dial, 1983. (New York)
80. *There's No Place Like Home.* (Palmer) Morrow, 1963. (Alaska)
81. *Kirk's Law.* (Peck) Doubleday, 1981. (Vermont)
82. *Cook Inlet Decision.* (Pedersen) Atheneum, 1963. (Alaska)
83. *Dangerous Flight.* (Pedersen) Abingdon Press, 1960. (Alaska)
84. *The World So Fair.* (Peyton) Chilton, 1963. (Minnesota)
85. *Fantasy Summer.* (Pfeffer) Pacer, 1984. (New York)
86. *Wiser Than Winter.* (Pitkin) Pantheon, 1960. (Vermont)
87. *Wipeout.* (Pomeroy) Four Winds, 1968. (Long Island)
88. *Edisto.* (Powell) Farrar, 1984. (South Carolina)
89. *The Yearling.* (Rawlings) Scribner's, 1967. (Florida)
90. *Summer of the Monkeys.* (Rawls) Doubleday, 1976. (Oklahoma)
91. *Rebels in the Shadows.* (Reilly) Bruce, 1962. (Pennsylvania)
92. *Summer at High Kingdom.* (Rich) Franklin Watts, 1975. (Maine)
93. *Light in the Forest.* (Richter) Knopf, 1953. (Delaware)
94. *Bright Island.* (Robinson) Random House, 1937. (Maine)
95. *Surfaces of a Diamond.* (Rubin) Louisiana St. Univ. Press, 1981. (South Carolina)
96. *Revolt along the Rio Grande.* Ryan Naylor, 1964. (New Mexico)
97. *Haunted.* (St. George) Bantam, 1980. (Pennsylvania)
98. *In the Shadow of the Bear.* (St. George) Putnam, 1983. (Alaska)
99. *Shane.* (Schaefer) Houghton, 1954. (Wyoming)
100. *Maybe Next Summer.* (Schellie) Four Winds, 1980. (Arizona)

101. *Stream Runner.* (Seed) Four Winds, 1979. (California)
102. *The Great Condominium Rebellion.* (Snyder) Delacorte, 1981. (Florida)
103. *Miracles on Maple Hill.* (Sorensen) Harcourt, 1956. (Pennsylvania)
104. *Witch of Blackbird Pond.* (Speare) Dell, 1958. (Connecticut)
105. *Tomahawk Border.* (Steele) Holt, Rinehart & Winston, 1966. (Virginia)
106. *The Year of the Bloody Sevens.* (Steele) Harcourt, Brace & World, 1963. (Kentucky)
107. *Of Mice and Men.* (Steinbeck) Bantam, 1970. (California)
108. *The Red Pony.* (Steinbeck) Bantam, 1967. (California)
109. *Tortilla Flat.* (Steinbeck) Collier, 1935. (California)
110. *The Perrely Plight.* (Stephens) Atheneum, 1965. (Massachusetts)
111. *Teetoncey.* (Taylor) Avon, 1975. (North Carolina)
112. *Tucker and the Horse Thief.* (Terris) Four Winds, 1979. (California)
113. *The Twelve Labors of Wimpole Stout.* (Webb) Abingdon Press, 1970. (Pennsylvania)
114. *How Long Is Always?* (Weber) Crowell, 1970. (Colorado)
115. *Lost Island.* (Whitney) Doubleday, 1970. (Georgia)
116. *The Loner.* (Wier) McKay, 1963. (Montana)
117. *Little House on the Prairie.* (Wilder) Harper & Row, 1953. (Kansas)
118. *Oh, Susanna.* (Williams) Putnam, 1963. (Kansas)
119. *And What of You, Josephine Charlotte?* (Witheridge) Atheneum, 1969. (Maryland)
120. *Patterns on the Wall.* (Yates) Dutton, 1943. (New Hampshire)
121. *Child of the Owl.* (Yep) Dell, 1977. (California)
122. *Here's Looking at You, Kid.* (Zalben) Farrar, 1984. (Long Island)

144. Fiction: Cities & Areas of the World

In the card catalog, locate fiction titles about cities and areas of the world. The do not have to mention the place in their titles.

1. *The Kraymer Mystery.* (Allan) Criterion, 1969. (New York City)
2. *Hell's Kitchen.* (Appel) Pantheon, 1977. (New York City)
3. *Green Street.* (Arundel) Hawthorn Books, 1970. (Edinburgh)
4. *Stranded; A Story of New York in 1875.* (Burchard) Coward-McCann, 1967. (New York City)
5. *Men of Athens.* (Coolidge) Houghton Mifflin, 1962. (Athens)
6. *Hilarion.* (Curley) Houghton Mifflin, 1979. (New York City)
7. *Killer Music.* (Eisenberg) Fearon Pitman, 1980. (London)
8. *A Spy in Old Detroit.* (Emery) Rand McNally, 1963. (Detroit)
9. *Six Blue Horses.* (Escoula) Phillips, 1970. (Paris)
10. *Second Son.* (Faulkner) Colonial Williamsburg, 1969. (London)
11. *A Stage for Rom.* (Faulkner) Doubleday, 1962. (Williamsburg, Virginia)
12. *Everybody but Me.* (First) Prentice, 1976. (Boston)
13. *Gang Girl.* (Fleischman) Doubleday, 1967. (New York City)
14. *Johnny Tremain.* (Forbes) Houghton Mifflin, 1943. (Boston)
15. *The Skies of Crete.* (Forman) Farrar, Straus, 1963. (Crete)
16. *Mrs. Mike.* (Freedman) Coward-McCann, 1947. (Alberta)
17. *Nantucket Summer.* (Green) Nelson, 1974. (Nantucket, Mass.)
18. *Foxy.* (Griffith) Greenwillow, 1984. (Florida Keys, Florida)
19. *Boris.* (Haar) Delacorte, 1969. (Leningrad)
20. *Home Boy.* (Hansen) Clarion, 1982. (Bronx, New York)
21. *Sea Star; Orphan of Chincoteague.* (Henry) Rand McNally, 1949. (Chincoteague Island)
22. *Jazz Country.* (Hentoff) Harper, 1965. (New York City)
23. *The Lion of the Kalahari.* (Hobson) Greenwillow, 1976. (Kalahari Desert)
24. *Slake's Limbo.* (Holman) Dell, 1974. (New York City)
25. *Les Miserables.* (Hugo) Random House, n.d.. (Paris)
26. *A Stranger Came Ashore.* (Hunter) Harper & Row, 1975. (Shetland Islands)
27. *Eleven! Time to Think of Marriage.* (Kalish) Atheneum, 1970. (Bengal)
28. *Me and My Million.* (King) Crowell, 1979. (London)
29. *You Are the Rain.* (Knudson) Dell, 1978. (Everglades, Fla.)

30. *Miles to Go.* (Kram) Morrow, 1982. (Boston)
31. *The People Therein.* (Lee) Clarion, 1980. (Appalachian Mountains)
32. *The Jade Amulet.* (Linton) Funk & Wagnalls, 1965. (Yucatan)
33. *Kallie's Corner.* (Low) Pantheon, 1966. (New York City)
34. *Teacup Full of Roses.* (Mathis) Viking, 1972. (Washington, D.C.)
35. *A Small Piece of Paradise.* (Morgan) Knopf, 1967. (London)
36. *The Young Landlords.* (Myers) Avon, 1979. (Harlem, New York)
37. *Fogarty.* (Neville) Harper, 1969. (New York City)
38. *It's Like This, Cat.* (Neville) Harper & Row, 1963. (New York City)
39. *The Seventeenth-Street Gang.* (Neville) Harper & Row, 1966. (New York City)
40. *Silver Chief, Dog of the North.* (O'Brien) Holt, Rinehart & Winston, 1933. (Arctic regions)
41. *The Black Pearl.* (O'Dell) Dell, 1967. (Baja, CA)
42. *Jacob Have I Loved.* (Paterson) Crowell, 1980. (Chesapeake Bay Region)
43. *Out at Home.* (Pomeranz) Houghton Mifflin, 1985. (Chicago)
44. *The Dog that Watched the Mountain.* (Price) Coward-McCann, 1967. (Alps)
45. *Apples Every Day.* (Richardson) Harper & Row, 1965. (Montreal)
46. *Calico Captive.* (Speare) Houghton Mifflin, 1957. (Montreal)
47. *London Snow: A Christmas Story.* (Theroux) Houghton Mifflin, 1979. (London)
48. *Three Against London.* (Varble) Doubleday, 1962. (London)
49. *The Eagles Have Flown.* (Williamson) Knopf, 1957. (Rome)
50. *Mystery of the Roman Ransom.* (Winterfeld) Harcourt, 1977. (Rome)
51. *Child of the Owl.* (Yep) Dell, 1977. (San Francisco)
52. *Little Women.* (Alcott) Little, 1968. (New England)
53. *The Mills of God.* (Armstrong) Doubleday, 1973. (Appalachian regions)
54. *North to Abilene.* (Ball) Holiday, 1960. (The West)

55. *Mercy Short: A Winter Journal, North Boston 1692–93.* (Faber) Dutton, 1982. (New England)
56. *A Gathering of Old Men.* (Gaines) Knopf, 1983. (The South)
57. *The Big Sky.* (Guthrie) Bantam, 1947. (The West)
58. *To Kill a Mockingbird.* (Lee) Lippincott, 1960. (The South)
59. *Me, Cholay & Co.; Apache Warriors.* (Schellie) Four Winds, 1973. (West)
60. *The Virginian.* (Wister) Childrens Press, 1968. (The West)

145. Fiction: Countries of the World

In the card catalog, locate fiction about countries of the world. The country does not have to be mentioned in the title.

1. *Gideon: A Novel.* (Aaron) Lippincot, 1982. (Poland)
2. *Black Hearts in Battersea.* (Aiken) Doubleday, 1964. (Great Britain)
3. *The Shadow Guests.* (Aiken) Delacorte, 1980. (England)
4. *The Stonewalkers.* (Alcock) Delacorte, 1983. (England)
5. *Signpost to Switzerland.* (Allan) Criterion, 1962. (Switzerland)
6. *The Violent Land.* (Amado) Knopf, 1965. (Brazil)
7. *The Journey of the Shadow Bairns.* (Anderson) Knopf, 1980. (Canada)
8. *Skin Diver.* (Ball) Holiday House, 1956. (Bahamas)
9. *The Little Minister.* (Barrie) Grosset, 1954. (Scotland)
10. *Tomorrow's Sphinx.* (Bell) Macmillan, 1986. (Egypt)
11. *The Ark.* (Benary-Isbert) Harcourt, Brace & World, 1953. (Germany)
12. *Rowan Farm.* (Benary-Isbert) Harcourt, Brace & World, 1954. (Germany)
13. *Under a Changing Moon.* (Benary-Isbert) Harcourt, 1964. (Germany)
14. *The Clue of the Black Cat.* (Berna) Pantheon, 1965. (France)
15. *The Knights of King Midas.* (Berna) Pantheon, 1961. (France)
16. *The Secret of the Missing Boat.* (Berna) Pantheon, 1967. (Brittany)
17. *The Severnside Mystery.* (Boden) McKay, 1970. (England)

18. *The Search of Mary Katherine Mulloy.* (Bolton) Nelson, 1974. (Ireland)
19. *The Seal of Jai.* (Booz) Macmillan, 1968. (India)
20. *Barracuda Gang.* (Bosse) Scholastic, 1982. (Caribbean)
21. *White Water, Still Water.* (Bosworth) Doubleday, 1966. (Canada)
22. *The Iron Roads.* (Bramble) St. Martins, 1981. (England)
23. *The Fox in Winter.* (Branfield) Atheneum, 1982. (England)
24. *The Incredible Journey.* (Burnford) Little, 1961. (Canada)
25. *Little Lord Fauntleroy.* (Burnett) Doubleday, 1954. (England)
26. *Riders of the Storm.* (Burton) Crowell, n.d.. (Great Britain)
27. *The Island of Helos.* (Butterworth) Pitman Learning, 1977. (Greece)
28. *Prisoner of Pedro Cay.* (Butterworth) Pitman Learning, 1980. (West Indies)
29. *The Sniper at Zimba.* (Butterworth) Pitman Learning, 1977. (Africa)
30. *The Mountain of Truth.* (Carlson) Atheneum, 1972. (Tibet)
31. *The Black Lamp.* (Carter) Nelson, 1973. (England)
32. *The Ghost of Ballyhooly.* (Cavanna) Morrow, 1971. (Ireland)
33. *Spice Island Mystery.* (Cavanna) Morrow, 1969. (West India)
34. *Stamp Twice for Murder.* (Cavanna) Morrow, 1981. (France)
35. *The Adventures of Don Quixote de la Mancha.* (Cervantes) Knopf, 1960. (Spain)
36. *Half a World Away.* (Chauncy) Watts, 1962. (Australia)
37. *High and Haunted Island.* (Chauncy) Norton, 1965. (Tasmania)
38. *A Love So Wild.* (Chester) Ballantine, 1981. (England)
39. *The Sign of the Owl.* (Chester) Four Winds, 1981. (France)
40. *Secret of the Andes.* (Clark) Viking, 1952. (Peru)
41. *The Tynedale Daughters.* (Clark) Walker, 1981. (England)
42. *A Boy Like Walt.* (Clewes) Coward-McCann, 1967. (Great Britain)
43. *The Cat Who Went to Heaven.* (Coatsworth) Macmillan, 1958. (Japan)
44. *The Wanderers.* (Coatsworth) Four Winds, 1972. (Ireland)
45. *Lottery in Lives.* (Couper) Houghton Mifflin, 1971. (Australia)

46. *Jungle Jenny.* (Cowen) Fearon Pitman, 1979. (Brazil)
47. *A Hanging at Tyburn.* (Cross) Atheneum, 1983. (England)
48. *Dear Rat.* (Cunningham) Avon, 1977. (France)
49. *Ghost Lane.* (Curry) Atheneum, 1979. (England)
50. *The Door in the Wall.* (De Angeli) Doubleday, 1949. (Great Britain)
51. *Transport 7-41-R.* (Degens) Viking, 1974. (Germany)
52. *Between Home and Horizon.* (DeJong) Knopf, 1962. (Holland)
53. *House of Sixty Fathers.* (DeJong) Harper, 1956. (China)
54. *The Wheel on the School.* (DeJong) Harper & Row, 1954. (Netherlands)
55. *The Names.* (DeLillo) Knopf, 1982. (Stories of other lands)
56. *Reina, the Galgo.* (De Messieres) Elsevier/Nelson, 1981. (Great Britain)
57. *A Christmas Carol in Prose.* (Dickens) Macmillan, 1963. (Great Britain)
58. *A Christmas Carol.* (Dickens) Pendulum Press, 1978. (Great Britain)
59. *David Copperfield.* (Dickens) Dodd, 1943. (England)
60. *Great Expectations.* (Dickens) Dodd, Mead, 1942. (England)
61. *The Life and Adventures of Nicholas Nickleby.* (Dickens) New American Library, 1982. (England)
62. *Oliver Twist.* (Dickens) Dodd, 1941. (England)
63. *A Tale of Two Cities.* (Dickens) Allyn and Bacon, 1922. (France)
64. *Annerton Pit.* (Dickinson) Little, Brown, 1977. (England)
65. *Tulku.* (Dickinson) Dutton, 1979. (Tibet)
66. *The Coriander.* (Dillon) Funk, 1964. (Ireland)
67. *Ragtime.* (Doctorow) Bantam, 1975. (U.S.)
68. *Hans Brinker.* (Dodge) World, 1946. (Netherlands)
69. *The Count of Monte Cristo.* (Dumas) Bantam, 1956. (France)
70. *The Man in the Iron Mask.* (Dumas) Pendulum Press, 1978. (France)
71. *Three Musketeers.* (Dumas) Grosset, 1953. (France)
72. *Rebecca.* (DuMaurier) Avon, 1971. (Great Britain)
73. *Three Complete Novels & Five Short Stories.* (DuMaurier) Avenel, 1981. (France)
74. *Guns at Quebec.* (Dwight) Macmillan, 1962. (Canada)

75. *Golden Idol.* (Eisenberg) Fearon Pitman, 1980. (China)
76. *The Moonlight Bride.* (Emecheta) Braziller, 1983. (Nigeria)
77. *Moonfleet.* (Falkner) Little, n.d.. (Great Britain)
78. *Bravo, Burro!* (Fante) Hawthorn Books, 1970. (Mexico)
79. *The Siege of Trapp's Mill.* (Farjeon) Atheneum, 1974. (England)
80. *Pashka of Bear Ravine.* (Fedoseyev) Pantheon, 1967. (Russia)
81. *A Russian Farewell.* (Fisher) Four Winds, 1980. (Russia)
82. *The Sea Broke Through.* (Flakkeberg) Knopf, 1959. (Netherlands)
83. *Three Complete Novels.* (Forsyth) Avenel, 1981. (Africa) (France)
84. *The French Lieutenant's Woman.* (Fowles) New American Library, 1969. (Great Britain)
85. *Mrs. Mike.* (Freedman) Coward-McCann, 1947. (Canada)
86. *The Strange Affair of Adelaide Harris.* (Garfield) Pantheon, 1971. (England)
87. *Adam of the Road.* (Gray) Viking Press, 1942. (Great Britain)
88. *Us: Inside a Teenage Gang.* (Green) Hastings House, 1982. (England)
89. *Boris.* (Haar) Delacorte, 1969. (Russia)
90. *The Return of the Native.* (Hardy) Pendulum, 1978. (Great Britain)
91. *Goodbye Mr. Chips.* (Hilton) Bantam, 1962. (Great Britain)
92. *Behind the Walls.* (Hobart) Funk & Wagnalls, 1961. (Mexico)
93. *The Lion of the Kalahari.* (Hobson) Greenwillow, 1976. (Africa)
94. *The Lion's Cub.* (Hoover) Four Winds, 1974. (Russia)
95. *The Night of the Scorpion.* (Horowitz) Berkley/Pacer, 1985. (Peru)
96. *The Nature of the Beast.* (Howker) Greenwillow, 1985. (England)
97. *Green Mansions.* (Hudson) Dodd, Mead, 1949. (Venezuela)
98. *The Second Heart.* (Hull) Atheneum, 1973. (Mexico)
99. *The Haunted Mountain.* (Hunter) Harper, 1972. (Scotland)
100. *A Sound of Chariots.* (Hunter) Avon, 1972. (Scotland)

101. *Follow Tomas.* (Hurd) Dial Press, 1963. (Greece)
102. *Mr. Murdock Takes Command; A Story of Pirates and Rebellion in Haiti.* (Icenhower) Winston, 1958. (Haiti)
103. *Don't Cry for Me.* (Jarunkova) Four Winds, 1968. (Czechoslovakia)
104. *Paulo and the Wolf.* (Jenkins) Criterion, 1963. (France)
105. *Gabriel's Girl.* (Johnston) Atheneum, 1983. (Spain)
106. *Indiana Jones & the Temple of Doom.* (Kahn) Ballantine, 1984. (India)
107. *Trumpeter of Krakow.* (Kelly) Macmillan, 1928. (Poland)
108. *Tunes of Glory.* (Kennaway) Harper, 1956. (Scotland)
109. *Success to the Brave.* (Kent) Putnam's, 1983. (England)
110. *All the Mowgli Stories.* (Kipling) Doubleday, 1936. (India)
111. *The Jungle Book.* (Kipling) Childrens Press, 1968. (India)
112. *Traveling with Oma.* (Kleberger) Atheneum, 1970. (Germany)
113. *Ghost Vision.* (Kortum) Pantheon, 1983. (Greenland)
114. *The Way of the Condor.* (Kravetz) Crown, 1970. (Peru)
115. *The Jade Gate.* (Lavolle) Abelard-Schuman, 1963. (China)
116. *The Dram Road.* (Lawrence) Harper & Row, 1983. (England)
117. *Star Lord.* (Lawrence) Harper & Row, 1978. (Wales)
118. *The Other Island.* (Leighton) Farrar, 1971. (Greece)
119. *Chain of Chance.* (Lem) Harcourt, Brace, 1978. (Italy)
120. *Dragons in the Water.* (L'Engle) Farrar, 1976. (Venezuela)
121. *Dive for the Sun.* (Love) Houghton Mifflin, 1982. (Peru)
122. *The Thorn Birds.* (McCullough) Avon, 1977. (Australia)
123. *A Dog Called Porridge.* (MacKellar) Dodd, Mead, 1985. (Scotland)
124. *River of Death.* (MacLean) Doubleday, 1981. (Brazil)
125. *Remi.* (Malot) Hawthorn Books, 1970. (France)
126. *Ali and the Ghost Tiger.* (Masters) Westminster, 1970. (Indonesia)
127. *The Sandy Shoe Mystery.* (Mooney) Lippincott, 1970. (Virgin Islands)
128. *The Quickenberry Tree.* (Motley) St. Martins, 1984. (Great Britain)
129. *The Treasure of Diogenes.* (Munves) Four Winds, 1979. (Columbia)

130. *Dogs of Fear; A Story of Modern Africa.* (Nagenda) Holt, 1972. (Africa) (Uganda)
131. *Village of the Vampire Cat.* (Namioka) Delacorte, 1981. (Japan)
132. *Megan.* (Noble) Messner, 1965. (Canada)
133. *The Top Step.* (Norris) Atheneum, 1970. (Sweden)
134. *Silver Chief, Dog of the North.* (O'Brien) Holt, Rinehart & Winston, 1933. (Canada)
135. *The Feathered Serpent.* (O'Dell) Houghton Mifflin, 1981. (Mexico)
136. *The Scarlet Pimpernel.* (Orczy) Putnam, n.d. (France)
137. *Doctor Zhivago.* (Pasternak) New American Library, 1958. (Russia)
138. *Rebels of the Heavenly Kingdom.* (Paterson) Avon, 1983. (China)
139. *Manuel's Discovery.* (Patton) McKay, 1970. (Bermuda) (Azores)
140. *Red Falcons of Tremaine.* (Peart) Random House, 1956. (Great Britain)
141. *Hurricane Weather.* (Pease) Doubleday, 1936. (Oceania)
142. *The Right-Hand Man.* (Peyton) Oxford Univ. Press, 1977. (England)
143. *Sing a Song of Ambush.* (Peyton) Platt & Munk, 1964. (Canada)
144. *The White Twilight.* (Polland) Holt, Rinehart & Winston, 1962. (Denmark)
145. *The Merry Adventures of Robin Hood.* (Pyle) Junior Deluxe Ed., n.d. (Great Britain)
146. *Daughter of the Mountains.* (Rankin) Pocket Books, 1976. (India) (Tibet)
147. *Over the Gate.* (Read) Houghton Mifflin, 1965. (England)
148. *Horse of Air.* (Rees) Methuen, 1980. (England)
149. *The Journey Back.* (Reiss) Harper & Row, 1987. (Netherlands)
150. *The Tide in the Attic.* (Rhijn) Criterion Books, 1961. (Holland)
151. *Ivanhoe.* (Scott) Prentice-Hall, 1962. (Great Britain)
152. *The Great Thirst.* (Seed) Bradbury, 1973. (Namibia) (Africa)

153. *The Good Master.* (Seredy) Viking, 1935. (Hungary)
154. *The Girl in the Grove; A Story of Suspense.* (Severn) Harper & Row, 1974. (Great Britain)
155. *Manwolf.* (Skurzynski) Houghton Mifflin, 1981. (Poland)
156. *Devil's Harvest.* (Slaughter) Doubleday, 1963. (Laos)
157. *Blackbriar.* (Sleator) Scholastic, 1972. (Great Britain)
158. *The Blue Dress.* (Smith) Dutton, 1962. (England)
159. *Gorky Park.* (Smith) Random House, 1981. (Russia)
160. *Free Ticket to Adventure.* (Soderhjelm) Lothrop, Lee & Shepherd, 1964. (Austria) (Scandinavia)
161. *Ash Road.* (Southall) St. Martins, 1965. (Australia)
162. *Hills End.* (Southall) Washington Square Press, 1962. (Australia)
163. *The Bronze Bow.* (Speare) Houghton, 1961. (Palestine)
164. *The Green Laurel.* (Spence) Roy Publishers, 1965. (Austria)
165. *Call It Courage.* (Sperry) Macmillan, 1940. (Polynesia)
166. *The Pearl.* (Steinbeck) Bantam, 1947. (Mexico)
167. *The Black Arrow; A Tale of the Two Roses.* (Stevenson) Dutton, 1965. (Great Britain)
168. *Kidnapped.* (Stevenson) Dodd, Mead, 1949. (Scotland)
169. *The Bushbabies.* (Stevenson) Houghton Mifflin, 1965. (Kenya)
170. *The Crystal Cave.* (Stewart) Fawcett, 1970. (Great Britain)
171. *The Red Lion.* (Stewart) G.P. Putnam's, 1960. (Scotland)
172. *Moses Beech.* (Strachan) Oxford University Press, 1983. (England)
173. *Thursday's Child.* (Streatfeild) Random House, 1970. (England)
174. *Uncle Misha's Partisans.* (Suhl) Four Winds, 1973. (Russia)
175. *Warrior Scarlet.* (Sutcliff) Walck, 1958. (Great Britain)
176. *Nikokenka's Childhood or Childhood.* (Tolstoy) Random House, 1930. (Russia)
177. *Good-bye to the Jungle.* (Townsend) Lippincott, 1965. (Great Britain)
178. *Mooncoin Castle; or Skulduggery Rewarded.* (Turkle) Viking, 1970. (Ireland)
179. *A Connecticut Yankee in King Arthur's Court.* (Twain) Harper & Row, 1917. (Great Britain)

180. *The Prince and the Pauper.* (Twain) Scott, 1956. (Great Britain)
181. *Banner in the Sky.* (Ullman) Lippincott, 1954. (Switzerland)
182. *Supermouse.* (Ure) Morrow, 1984. (England)
183. *When Half-Gods Go.* (Valencak) Morrow, 1976. (Greece)
184. *The Secret of Belledonne Room 16.* (Vries) McGraw-Hill, 1979. (France)
185. *Talking in Whispers.* (Watson) Knopf, 1983. (Chile)
186. *Lark.* (Watson) Holt, 1964. (Great Britain)
187. *The Awakening.* (Wayne) Grosset, 1972. (Russia)
188. *Mystery in Newfoundland.* (Wees) Abelard-Schuman, 1965. (Newfoundland)
189. *Red Sails to Capri.* (Weil) Viking, 1952. (Italy)
190. *Wet Fire.* (Wheeler) Childrens Press, 1977. (Borneo)
191. *No Man's Land.* (White) Doubleday, 1969. (Islands of the Pacific)
192. *Philippine Islands Surrender.* (White) Doubleday, 1966. (Philippines)
193. *Secret of the Samurai Sword.* (Whitney) Westminster Press, 1958. (Japan)
194. *The King's Beard.* (Wibberley) Farrar, Straus, 1952. (Great Britain)
195. *The Bridge of San Luis Rey.* (Wilder) Grosset, 1927. (Peru)
196. *Storm from the West.* (Willard) Harcourt, 1964. (Scotland)
197. *The Tunnel.* (Williams) Abelard-Schuman, 1961. (Poland)
198. *The Iron Charm.* (Williamson) Knopf, 1964. (Europe)
199. *Jacobin's Daughter.* (Williamson) THP, 1981. (France)
200. *To Dream Upon a Crown.* (Williamson) Knopf, 1967. (Great Britain)
201. *On Firm Ice.* (Wilson) Crowell, 1970. (Canada)
202. *Shadow of a Bull.* (Wojciechowska) Atheneum, 1972. (Spain)
203. *Beau Geste.* (Wren) Lippincott, 1925. (France) (Africa)

146. Books Made into Movies

In the card catalog, find as many fiction titles as you can that have been made into movies:

Author	Title
Adams	Watership Down
Alcott	Little Women
Anson	Amityville Horror
Austen	Pride and Prejudice
Bagnold	National Velvet
Benchley	Jaws
Black	Raiders of the Lost Ark
Boulle	Bridge Over the River Kwai
Braithwaite	To Sir, With Love
Burdick	Fail-Safe
Burnett	Little Lord Fauntleroy
Carroll	Alice in Wonderland / Through the Looking Glass
Christie	Evil Under the Sun
Collodi	Pinocchio
Cook	Coma
Cooper	The Last of the Mohicans
Crane	Red Badge of Courage
Davies	Miracle on 34th Street
Defoe	Robinson Crusoe
Dickens	A Christmas Carol
Dickens	David Copperfield
Dickens	Oliver Twist
Dickens	Tale of Two Cities
Dickey	Deliverance
Dodge	Hans Brinker
Dostoyevsky	Crime and Punishment
Douglas	The Robe
Doyle	Adventures of Sherlock Holmes
Doyle	Hound of the Baskervilles
Dumas	The Count of Monte Cristo
Dumas	The Three Musketeers
DuMaurier	Rebecca
Fleischer	Annie
Follett	Eye of the Needle

Forsyth	Odessa File (Three Complete Novels)
Fowles	The French Lieutenant's Woman
Frank	Ann Frank, Diary of a Young Girl
Freedman	Mrs. Mike
Gaines	The Autobiography of Miss Jane Pittman
Gallico	The Poseidon Adventure
Gilbreth	Cheaper by the Dozen
Gipson	Old Yeller
Heller	Catch 22
Hemingway	Old Man and the Sea
Herbert	Dune
Hilton	Goodbye Mr. Chips
Hudson	Green Mansions
Hugo	Les Miserables
Irving	The Legend of Sleepy Hollow
Johnston	Happy Days No. 4; Fonzie, Fonzie, Superstar
Johnston	Welcome Back Kotter; Barbarino Drops Out
Kahn	Indiana Jones and the Temple of Doom
Kahn	Return of the Jedi
Kellogg	Tell Me That You Love Me, Junie Moon
King	Carrie
King	Christine
King	Cujo
King	The Shining
Lee	To Kill a Mockingbird
Levin	The Boys from Brazil
Lofting	The Voyages of Doctor Dolittle
London	Call of the Wild
Lucas	Star Wars

McCullough	Thorn Birds
Melville	Moby Dick
Michener	Bridges at Toko-Ri
Michener	Hawaii
Nolan	Logan's Run
Nordhoff & Hall	Mutiny on the Bounty
Orczy	The Scarlet Pimpernel
Pasternak	Doctor Zhivago
Roddenberry	Star Trek: The Motion Picture
Scott	Ivanhoe
Smith	Gorky Park
Steinbeck	Of Mice and Men
Stevenson	Dr. Jekyll and Mr. Hyde
Stevenson	Kidnapped
Stevenson	Treasure Island
Stoker	Dracula
Stowe	Uncle Tom's Cabin
Twain	Connecticut Yankee in King Arthur's Court
Twain	Tom Sawyer
Verne	Around the World in Eighty Days
Verne	Journey to the Center of the Earth
Verne	Twenty Thousand Leagues Under the Sea
Wallace	Ben Hur
Weatherby	Chariots of Fire
Wilder	Little House on the Prairie
Wren	Beau Geste

III. QUIET MENTAL GAMES

147. *Alphabet Fiction Titles*

Name a fiction title beginning with each letter of the alphabet. (Hint: Only one of the titles below is from a short story collection.)

A—*And Now Miguel*—(Krumgold)
B—*Bridge to Terabithia*—(Paterson)
C—*Call It Courage*—(Sperry)
D—*Dicey's Song*—(Voigt)
E—*The Enchanted*—(Coatsworth)
F—*Fear Rides High*—(Heavilen)
G—*Good-Bye My Shadow*—(Stolz)
H—*Hospital Zone*—(Stolz)
I—*If You Could See What I Hear*—(Sullivan)
J—*Joyride*—(Cavanna)
K—*Kate's Story*—(Leach)
L—*Listen, the Drum*—(Alter)
M—*My Sweet Audrina*—(Andrews)
N—*Noonday Friends*—(Stolz)
O—*Onion John*—(Krumgold)
P—*Praise All the Moons of Morning*—(Stone)
Q—*The Quickenberry Tree*—(Motley)
R—*Rabbit Hill*—(Lawson)
S—*The Sea Wolf*—(London)
T—*Tuck Everlasting*—(Babbitt)
U—*Uncle Tom's Cabin*—(Stowe)
V—*Viva Chicano*—(Bonham)
W—*A Watcher in the Woods*—(Randall)

X — *"X-ing a Paragrab"* — (Poe) from The Complete Tales &
    Poems of Edgar Allan Poe
Y — *Your Bird Is Here, Tom Thompson* — (Wood)
Z — *Zia* — (O'Dell)

148. Family Situations

In the card catalog, locate fiction titles about family situations.
Find those that will spell out "FAMILY SITUATIONS" with their first
letters.

F — *Fog* — (Lee)
A — *Almost Like Sisters* — (Cavanna)
M — *Mom, the Wolf Man and Me* — (Klein)
I — *The Immigrants* — (Fast)
L — *Look Through My Window* — (Little)
Y — *Young Unicorns* — (L'Engle)

S — *Sweet Whispers, Brother Rush* — (Hamilton)
I — *In Real Life, I'm Just Kate* — (Morgenroth)
T — *Toby Alone* — (Branscum)
U — *Up a Road Slowly* — (Hunt)
A — *Anastasia Krupnik* — (Lowry)
T — *Temporary Times* — (Robinson)
I — *Incident at Hawk's Hill* — (Eckert)
O — *Of Time and of Seasons* — (Johnston)
N — *None of the Above* — (Wells)
S — *Summer of the Monkeys* — (Rawls)

149. A Fishy Riddle

Name the fish that:

1. rhymes with doubt. (trout)
2. rhymes with sounder, and means to pause. (flounder)
3. rhymes with seal. (eel)
4. is dangerous and rhymes with lark. (shark)

5. is an old naggy woman. (hagfish)
6. is a paddle. (oarfish)
7. has wings, and comes from Heaven. (angelfish)
8. is a male pig. (hogfish)
9. is a furry feline pet. (catfish)
10. is an orange-pink color. (salmon)

150. *What Is Meant?*

What word ends with "-ment," and means:

1. growth? (development)
2. indifference? (detachment)
3. consequences? (punishment)
4. disposition? (temperament)
5. including? (involvement)
6. captivity? (confinement)
7. beginning? (commencement)
8. betterment? (improvement)
9. success? (accomplishment)
10. surprise? (astonishment)
11. employment? (appointment)
12. acquisition? (attainment)
13. fun? (merriment)
14. inactivity? (retirement)
15. division? (department)

151. *Fiction Fun I*

What fiction book title reminds you of:

1. fat? (*Blimp* — Cavallaro)
2. a fat man? (*The Pigman* — Zindel)
3. a snake? (*Fer-de-Lance* — Stout)
4. the green charm? (*The Jade Amulet* — Linton)
5. a house plus little fellow? (*Home Boy* — Hansen)
6. small grownup girls? (*Little Women* — Alcott)

7.   an ocean wild dog? (*The Sea Wolf*—London)
8.   a Christmas song? (*A Christmas Carol*—Dickens)
9.   phantom road? (*Ghost Lane*—Curry)
10.   a cat and sight? (*Tiger Eyes*—Blume)
11.   mug full of flowers? (*Teacup Full of Roses*—Mathis)
12.   almost 16 plus one? (*Practically Seventeen*—Du Jardin)
13.   cloud? (*Fog*—Lee)
14.   a bear? (*The Grizzly*—Johnson)
15.   a wrap? (*The Robe*—Douglas)
16.   the opposite of sit? (*The Stand*—King)
17.   it rhymes with nesting plus play? (*The Westing Game*—Raskin)
18.   my dear, my meat sandwich? (*My Darling, My Hamburger*—Zindel)
19.   six plus two relatives? (*Eight Cousins*—Alcott)
20.   one who doles out? (*The Giver*—Hall)

152. *Fiction Fun II*

What fiction book sounds like:

1.   a pigment between red and blue? (*The Color Purple*—Walker)
2.   a feline's crib? (*Cat's Cradle*—Vonnegut)
3.   a pungent herb plus dessert? (*Ginger Pye*—Estes)
4.   the opposite of light plus a ship? (*The Dark Frigate*—Hawes)
5.   a girl's name that sounds like precious gems plus a bunch of wild dogs? (*Julie of the Wolves*—George)
6.   a musical instrument of the horn family plus a dangerous drug plus a mature female of cattle? (*The Trumpeter of Krakow*—Kelly)
7.   a ruler of a country plus of the breeze? (*King of the Wind*—Henry)
8.   a distinct calmness? (*A Separate Peace*—Knowles)
9.   a dense lustrous growth in mollusks used as a gem? (*The Pearl*—Steinbeck)
10.   Mrs. plus a disc used in lazy afternoon play plus rodents plus

of plus the 14th letter of the alphabet, the 9th letter of the alphabet, the 13th letter of the alphabet, and the 8th letter of the alphabet? (*Mrs. Frisby and the Rats of NIMH* — O'Brien)

11. the opposite of down plus a path plus the opposite of fast? (*Up a Road Slowly* — Hunt)

12. the first season of the year plus of the large cat? (*The Spring of Tiger* — Holt)

13. the opposite of day plus a popular winter sport? (*The Night Skiers* — Bastien)

14. the opposite of before plus the beginning plus the opposite of life? (*After the First Death* — Cormier)

15. a story plus a couple of towns? (*Tale of Two Cities* — Dickens)

16. the fourth month plus early in the day? (*April Morning* — Fast)

17. to lug or take with you? (*Carrie* — King)

18. a light ax used by the Indians plus a boundary? (*Tomahawk Border* — Steele)

19. a small carnivorous pet plus in the reflective glass? (*Cat in the Mirror* — Stolz)

20. the 11th letter of the alphabet? (*The Cay* — Taylor)

153. Mary

Using a dictionary or thesaurus, name the "Mary" . . .

1. in a long race? (marathon)
2. in a percussion instrument like a gourd? (maraca)
3. in the usual? (customary)
4. in a flower related to the daisy with a yellow head? (marigold)
5. that makes meat taste good? (marinate)
6. in an herb from the mint family? (rosemary)
7. in a narcotic weed? (marijuana)
8. in a puppet? (marionette)
9. who navigates a ship? (mariner)
10. in a state? (Maryland)

154. State Savvy

Which of the states of the United States ...

1. is a girl's name? (Georgia, Virginia [West], Carolina even)
2. is a type of potato? (Idaho)
3. is the first president of the United States? (Washington)
4. is the opposite of old plus a Spanish-speaking country? (New Mexico)
5. is an exclamation plus a greeting plus an exclamation? (Ohio)
6. is a girl's first name plus territory? (Maryland)
7. is the first Americans plus the first letter of the alphabet? (Indiana)
8. is the opposite direction of east plus a feminine name? (West Virginia)
9. is what cars travel on plus an isolated land? (Rhode Island)
10. is to be sick plus it rhymes with toy? (Illinois)

155. River Ragbag

What major river in North America reminds you of the following?

1. a dairy product we drink? (Milk)
2. a beautiful and precious jewel? (Pearl)
3. harmony and calm? (Peace)
4. a complementary color of red? (Green)
5. a hole in space? (Black)
6. a lizard? (Gila)
7. a primary and hot color? (Red)
8. a city in Georgia? (Savannah)
9. a type of tree? (Cedar)
10. the opposite of South plus a dish? (North Platte)
11. an animal with sharp bristles? (Porcupine)
12. make-up or use it after your bath? (Powder)
13. a reptile? (Snake)
14. it means three? (Trinity)
15. the opposite of black? (White)

16. it is bigger than a stone? (Rock)
17. a famous English war leader? (Churchill)
18. a metal burrow? (Coppermine)
19. an Indian tribe? (Cheyenne)
20. a sunny color plus a rock? (Yellowstone)

156. Trees

What state tree reminds you of:

1. a lovely smelling southern flower? (magnolia — Mississippi)
2. a nut? (pecan — Texas)
3. how a male deer sees? (buckeye — Ohio)
4. it lost all hair? (bald cypress — Louisiana)
5. a vegetable? (cabbage palm — Florida)
6. a primary color plus a newborn plant? (redbud — Oklahoma)
7. something we drink? (Kentucky coffeetree — Kentucky)
8. a Christmas plant? (American holly — Delaware)
9. a country? (Norway pine — Minnesota)

157. Sea Race

How many kinds of "sea" can you find?

1. a sea that is to be sat in? (seat)
2. a sea that is safe for a voyage? (seaworthy)
3. a sea that is in the direction toward the open sea? (seaward)
4. a sea that is a starfish? (seastar)
5. a sea that is ill? (seasick)
6. a sea that is not elegant? (seamy)
7. a sea that is a spiritualist meeting? (séance)
8. a sea that looks for something? (search)
9. a sea that sounds like a canine? (seadog)
10. a sea that has lower appendages? (sealegs)
11. a sea that initials the construction battalion of the United States Navy? (SeaBee)
12. a sea that marks or certifies a paper? (seal)

13. a sea animal that is half fish and half horse? (seahorse)
14. a sea plant or alga? (seaweed)
15. a sea that is a spice or relish? (seasoning)

158. Stay for Tea?

How many kinds of "tea" can you recognize?

1. forever? (eternity)
2. having fun with a group? (party)
3. a worry? (anxiety)
4. heat and light source? (electricity)
5. a human hand or foot? (extremity)
6. worthy? (dignity)
7. uninterrupted connection? (continuity)
8. kidnapped? (captivity)
9. many people live there? (city)
10. cold tea? (frigidity)
11. a short tea? (brevity)
12. your national heritage? (nationality)
13. the whole amount? (totality)
14. finding valuables without trying? (serendipity)
15. medium tea? (mediocrity)

159. Bird Babble

Name the bird that reminds you of:

1. an advisor to the Pope. (cardinal)
2. a cookie. (oriole)
3. it captures annoying household insects. (flycatcher)
4. it races down the street. (roadrunner)
5. a tool that bangs nails plus a sunny color. (yellowhammer)
6. it ridicules. (mockingbird)
7. it does not whistle, nor sing, but.... (hummingbird)
8. it is a little crazy. (cuckoo)
9. a sneaky feline. (catbird)

10. a famous nurse, Florence's last name. (nightingale)
11. a girl's first name. (robin)
12. it gnaws at trees. (woodpecker)
13. the darkest color. (blackbird)
14. a group of islands off the northwest coast of Africa. (canary)

160. The "K" Game

Ask each member of the English class to find a word in the dictionary or the thesaurus that begins with "K" and contains two letters; three letters; four letters; and so on. The student who has the longest word wins. Definitions of the words must be given.

1. a two-letter word meaning a knockout in boxing. (KO)
2. a three-letter word meaning family. (kin)
3. a four-letter word meaning to intertwine. (knit)
4. a five-letter word meaning scoundrel. (knave)
5. a six-letter word meaning to ignite. (kindle)
6. a seven-letter word meaning perceptive. (knowing)
7. an eight-letter word meaning stunning. (knockout)
8. a nine-letter word meaning education. (knowledge)
9. a ten-letter word meaning chivalry. (knighthood)
10. an eleven-letter word meaning sympathetic. (kindhearted)
11. a twelve-letter word meaning a first class in school. (kindergarten)
12. a thirteen-letter word meaning everchanging. (kaleidoscopic)
13. a fourteen-letter word meaning knee-length pants. (knickerbockers)

161. Magazine Madness

Name a magazine that reminds you of:

1. the third and seventeenth letter of the alphabet. (*CQ*)
2. drama. (*Plays*)
3. what you do when you chew. (*Byte Magazine*)
4. recent past events. (*Current History*)

5. soil cycle. (*Dirt Bike*)
6. a precaution. (*Prevention*)
7. to uncover. (*Discover*)
8. a math tutor. (*Arithmetic Teacher*)
9. to count down and to meet. (*3-2-1 Contact*)
10. the area above the earth's atmosphere and a globe. (*Space World*)
11. one's surroundings. (*Environment*)
12. the center. (*Focus*)
13. invention or origination. (*Coinage*)
14. to hear. (*Listen*)
15. crazy. (*Mad*)
16. to dare. (*Challenge*)
17. tomorrow. (*Futurist*)
18. a preservationist. (*Conservationist*)
19. a bike. (*Cycle*)
20. the study of the stars. (*Astronomy*)

162. *Newbery Authors Rhyme*

What Newbery Award–winning author rhymes with the following?

1. yield? (Field)
2. pegs? (Meigs)
3. laws? (Hawes)
4. super? (Cooper)
5. lox? (Fox)
6. ames? (James)
7. fires? (Byars)
8. punt? (Hunt)
9. bee long? (De Jong)
10. singer? (Finger)
11. belly? (Kelly)
12. has pin? (Raskin)
13. pan spoon? (Van Loon)
14. lawyer? (Sawyer)
15. seethe? (Keith)

16. say? (Gray)
17. Oh Nell? (O'Dell)
18. berry? (Sperry)
19. dates? (Yates)
20. hear? (Speare)

163. Cars

Which car . . .

1. was the 16th president of the United States? (Lincoln)
2. was the 38th president of the United States? (Ford)
3. was where the pilgrims landed? (Plymouth)
4. was an Indian chief of the Ottawa tribe? (Pontiac)
5. swerves away? (Dodge)
6. was a Roman messenger of the Gods? (Mercury)
7. is the opposite of new plus the opposite of stationary? (Oldsmobile)
8. sounds like crying? (Saab)
9. is a member of the cat family? (Jaguar)
10. is the 2nd, 13th, and 23rd letter of the alphabet? (BMW)

164. Discovery of Nations

How many words with the ending "-nation" can you list?

1. a joining? (combination)
2. a censoring or blaming? (condemnation)
3. the summit? (culmination)
4. a slaying? (assassination)
5. hatred? (abomination)
6. superiority? (predomination)
7. to have named before? (prenomination)
8. control? (domination)
9. appointment? (nomination)
10. a threat? (commination)

165. Are You Able?

What word has the suffix "-able"?

1. safe for swallowing? (drinkable)
2. can become smaller and contracted? (shrinkable)
3. can be blamed? (culpable)
4. tolerable? (bearable)
5. cannot be pondered? (unthinkable)
6. cannot be submerged? (unsinkable)
7. can be shattered? (breakable)
8. can be outlined or made distinct? (definable)
9. can be put together? (combinable)
10. can descend? (declinable)

166. Magazine Scramble

Unscramble the names of these magazines.

1. M T E I. (*Time*)
2. T Y O M S C C O R T L I. (*Motorcyclist*)
3. E A ' S E R R D G I T S D E. (*Reader's Digest*)
4. E N E T. (*Teen*)
5. H A M O I S T I N S N. (*Smithsonian*)
6. 1-3-2 N A T T O C C. (*3-2-1 Contact*)
7. O N E B Y. (*Ebony*)
8. R P O S S T T U L A D I E T R S L. (*Sports Illustrated*)
9. O D O U O T R F I E L. (*Outdoor Life*)
10. T O R O M N E D R T. (*Motor Trend*)
11. N E E S V E T N E. (*Seventeen*)
12. L O P U R A P E N I S E C C. (*Popular Science*)
13. L A N T O A N I P E G I H O A R C G Z A M I G E A N. (*National Geographic Magazine*)
14. 0 8 R I M O C. (*80 Micro*)
15. G I S I N K. (*Skiing*)

167. *Book Title Scramble*

Unscramble the titles of these books. Name the author.

1. E D ' Y S I C   O G N S. (*Dicey's Song* — Voigt)
2. H E T   L O D   N M A   N A D   E H T   E S A. (*The Old Man and the Sea* — Hemingway)
3. R O D L   F O   H E T   S I L E F. (*Lord of the Flies* — Golding)
4. E T H   A E V L S   N C D E R A. (*The Slave Dancer* — Fox)
5. H T E   T E N I S G W   M G E A. (*The Westing Game* — Raskin)
6. L A E V G I L   F O   H E T   P A M E V R I   A T C. (*Village of the Vampire Cat* — Namioka)
7. H E T   B O B T I H. (*The Hobbit* — Tolkien)
8. E H T   G H H I   N I G K. (*The High King* — Alexander)
9. T E W I H   N A G F. (*White Fang* — London)
10. L A K E B   U H S O E. (*Bleak House* — Dickens)
11. T A C ' S   D R C L E A. (*Cat's Cradle* — Vonnegut)
12. P U   A   A R O D   W S Y L L O. (*Up a Road Slowly* — Hunt)
13. T E H   C T W H I   F O   B A R B L I C D K   D N O P. (*The Witch of Blackbird Pond* — Speare)
14. H E T   A P R E L. (*The Pearl* — Steinbeck)
15. G I K N   F O   H E T   D I W N. (*King of the Wind* — Henry)

168. *Cities*

What city reminds you of:

1. an indoors sport played with a ball plus the complementary color to red? (Bowling Green, Ky.)
2. the discoverer of America? (Columbus, Oh.)
3. the opposite of old plus a place to buy delicious food? (New Delhi, India)
4. where Napoleon's famous battle took place? (Waterloo, La.)

5. a room in the house? (Kitchener, Ontario)
6. a small animal with a hard shell beginning with the letter A? (Amarillo, Tex.)
7. what one uses to unlock a lock plus the opposite of east? (Key West, Fla.)
8. wild oxen? (Buffalo, N.Y.)
9. a struggle plus a stream of water? (Battle Creek, Mich.)
10. the eastern United States ocean? (Atlantic City, N.J.)
11. the second letter of the alphabet plus what a boy is to his father? (Tucson, Ariz.)
12. an Indian tribe in Arizona? (Pueblo, Col.)
13. the opposite of peace plus the past tense of see? (Warsaw, Poland)
14. one makes a sculpture with a plaster of. . .? (Paris, France)
15. rhymes with honkers? (Yonkers, N.Y.)
16. opposite of old plus a place of safety? (New Haven, Ct.)
17. the part of the sea coming into the land plus where ships stop? (Gulfport, Miss.)
18. scary? (Erie, Pa.)
19. the body of a ship? (Hull, Quebec)
20. a kind of tree plus swiftly moving water? (Cedar Rapids, Ia.)

IV. CONTESTS AND ACTIVE GAMES

169. Switchabout

Upon coming to the library media center, the English class is divided into five groups, and each group is given a copy of five questions in one category. The students will complete the questions given to their group and go on to the next section of questions. The five sections are Card Catalog; *Abridged Readers' Guide to Periodical Literature*; Reference; Nonfiction; and Fiction. Use the following questions, or make up your own:

FICTION

1. Find one fiction book on werewolves. Name title and author.
   answer: *Manwolf* by Gloria Skurzynski

2. What fiction book did Dale Carlson write?
   answer: *The Mountain of Truth*

3. Who is the author of *Night of the Prom*?
   answer: Debra Spector

4. Name a fiction book about ghosts by Richard Peck.
   answer: *The Ghosts Belonged to Me; A Novel; Ghosts I Have Been*

5. Find a fiction book about Tibet. Name title and author.
   answer: *Tulku* by Peter Dickinson

NONFICTION

1. What is the call number of the book *A Guide to Nature Projects*?
   answer: 574
           Pe

2. What nonfiction book did Dale Carlson write?
   answer: *Girls Are Equal, Too*

3. Where would one find a book on the Quechua Indians?
   answer: 980.3
           Man

4. Find a book on writing careers. What is the call number, author, and title?
   answer: Career   Gurney Williams *Writing Careers*
           070.023
           Wil

5. Name a book on villages found in the card catalog. Give the call number.
   answer: *Early Village Life* 307.7
           Kal

CARD CATALOG

1. How many pages is the book *The Last Battle* by Leonard Wibberley?
   answer: 197p.

2. What subject headings are listed under the book *Discovery of North America* by Michele Byam?
   answer: (1). U.S.-History (2). America-Discovery and Exploration

3. Who is the publisher for the book *The Battle of the Bulge* by American Heritage?
   answer: Harper & Row

4. What is the copyright date of the book *Night Talks* by Patricia Gauch?
   answer: 1983

5. What book did Pete Pomeroy write?
   answer: *Wipeout*

ABRIDGED READERS' GUIDE TO PERIODICAL LITERATURE

1. What does the abbreviation "il" mean?
   answer: illustration(s)

2. Find *two* magazine articles on rock concerts. Write down: a. the name of the magazine; b. the title of the article; c. the date of the magazine; and d. pages.

3. Find an article on cholesterol. Who is the author?

4. What magazine is abbreviated "Sch Update"?
   answer: Scholastic Update

5. Find one article on golf. Write down: a. the name of the magazine; b. the title of the article; c. the date of the magazine; and d. pages.

REFERENCE

1. Who said: "Good fences make good neighbors"?
   answer: Robert Frost. *Magill's Quotations in Context,* Magill, ed., p. 313. Look under neighbors in Key Word Index. R

   808.88
   Ma

2. Who was Blair Niles?
   answer: An American explorer and writer. *Webster's Biographical Dictionary,* Merriam-Webster, p. 1102. R

   920
   Web

3. What is and where is "Pemba"?
   answer: an island in Indian Ocean off NE coast of Tanganyika, E. Africa. *Webster's Geographical Dictionary,* Merriam-Webster, p. 866. R

   910
   Web

4. In the Zodiac, what is the English name for Aries?

answer: the Ram. *World Almanac and Book of Facts,* 1987,
p. 720. R
>   031
>   Wor

5.   What is a synonym for "munificent"?
     answer: generous, bountiful, liberal. *The Doubleday Roget's Thesaurus in Dictionary Form,* Landau, p. 444. R
>   423
>   Lan

170. *Recognition*

Do you recognize from which famous fiction book the following have been taken?

1.   He was born in the stables of the Sultan of Morocco. (*King of the Wind*—Henry)
2.   a bullfighter. (*Shadow of a Bull*—Wojciechowska)
3.   the trumpet is a symbol of heroism. (*The Trumpeter of Krakow*—Kelly)
4.   a samurai. (*Village of the Vampire Cat*—Namioka)
5.   Sunset Towers. (*The Westing Game*—Raskin)
6.   Wethersfield, Connecticut. (*The Witch of Blackbird Pond*—Speare)
7.   a Tesseract. (*A Wrinkle in Time*—L'Engle)
8.   the Mississippi River. (*The Adventures of Tom Sawyer*—Twain)
9.   Renfield. (*Dracula*—Stoker)
10. Bilbo Baggins. (*The Hobbit*—Tolkien)
11. David Balfour. (*Kidnapped*—Stevenson)
12. conch shell. (*Lord of the Flies*—Golding)
13. the marlin. (*The Old Man and the Sea*—Hemingway)
14. a scorpion. (*The Pearl*—Steinbeck)
15. Billy Bones. (*Treasure Island*—Stevenson)
16. Philip Marsham. (*The Dark Frigate*—Hawes)
17. the Spanish court. (*I, Juan de Pareja*—Trevino)
18. Chesapeake Bay. (*Jacob Have I Loved*—Paterson)

19. Alaska. (*Julie of the Wolves*—George)
20. Heathcliff. (*Wuthering Heights*—Bronte)

171. *Scavenger Hunt #1*

1. Find *The Doubleday Roget's Thesaurus in Dictionary Form* (R 423 Lan). Find a synonym, or a word that has a similar meaning, to "insolent."

> answer: impertinent, discourteous, disrespectful, rude, insulting, arrogant (p. 353)

2. Find *Van Nostrand's Scientific Encyclopedia* (R 503 Van). What is cuprum?

> answer: copper (p. 463)

3. Find the *Dictionary of American History*: Volume V. (973.03 Ada). Who were the Taënsa?

> answer: a small Indian tribe dwelling at Lake St. Joseph on the western bank of the Mississippi (p. 216)

4. Find *The World Almanac 1987* (R 031 Wor). When was Lucie Arnaz born? (Look for actors, actresses in index)

> answer: 7/17/51 (p. 400)

5. Find *The Guinness Book of World Records 1984* (R 032 Gui). What is the record for eating the most baked beans?

> answer: 2,780 cold beans one by one, with a cocktail stick, in 30 minutes by Karen Stevenson of Merseyside, England, April 4, 1981.

6. Find *Cassell's French Dictionary* (R 443 Gir). How do you spell the French word for order?

> answer: ordre (p. 355)

7. Find *Rand McNally Illustrated Dictionary of Sports* (R 796 Wri). In horse racing, how old is an "aged" horse considered to be?

> answer: 6 or more years old (p. 74)

8. Find *Magill's Quotations* (R 808.88 Mag). Who said: "Beauty is truth, truth is beauty"?

> answer: John Keats (p. 79)

9.　Find *Webster's Biographical Dictionary* (R 920 Web). Who was Thomas Huxley?

　　answer: English biologist (p. 751)

10.　Find *Webster's Geographical Dictionary* (R 910 Web). What and where is the "Sappa"?

　　answer: a river about 150 miles long Northwest Kansas and Southwest Nebraska (p. 1007)

172. Scavenger Hunt #2

1.　Find the *World Almanac 1987* (R 031 Wor). Look at the index in front of the book. Look under Honolulu, Hawaii. What is the tallest building in Honolulu, Hawaii? How many feet high is it? How many stories is it?

　　answers: p. 686. (tallest building — Ala Moana Americana Hotel; 396 ft. high, with 38 stories)

2.　Find *The Civil War Dictionary* (R 973.703 Boa). Who was Daniel Cameron?

　　answer: p. 115. (a Union officer)

3.　Find *The Encyclopedia of Sports* (R 796.03 Men). Find bobsledding in the index. What was the bobsled made from in ancient times?

　　answer: p. 192. (a strip of animal skin stretched between smoothed straps of wood)

4.　Find *Webster's Geographical Dictionary* (R 910 Web). What is the "Nith"?

　　answer: p. 791. (a river about 65 miles long in Southwest Scotland)

5.　Find *Breeding Aquarium Fishes* (R 639 Axe). Find the Desert Pupfish in the *Table of Contents*. In what countries is the desert pupfish found?

　　answer: p. 61. (Brazil and Africa)

6.　Find the *McGraw-Hill Dictionary of the Life Sciences* (R 570 Lap). What is the ego?

　　answer: p. 267. (the self. the conscious part of the personality that is in contact with reality)

173. *Scavenger Hunt #3*

1. Find *Cassell's Italian Dictionary,* Rebora (R 453 Reb). What is a "romanzo"?

    answer: p. 439. a novel; romance.

2. Find *Webster's Biographical Dictionary,* Merriam-Webster (R 920 Web). Who was Seth Boyden? What did he do?

    answer: p. 182. American inventer; invented process for making patent leather; malleable cast iron; sheet iron; a hat-shaping machine; manufactured locomotives.

3. Find the *Reader's Encyclopedia,* Benet (R 803 Ben). What is "Miss Thompson"?

    answer: p. 675. a short story by W. Somerset Maugham.

4. Find *A Dictionary of Battles,* Eggenberger (R 904 Egg). In what war did "Groveton" take place?

    answer: p. 179. American Civil War.

5. Find *Magill's Quotations in Context*, Magill (R 808.88 Ma). Who said "The very pink of perfection"?

    answer p. 1087. Oliver Goldsmith.

6. Find *The Doubleday Roget's Thesaurus in Dictionary Form*, Landau (R 423 Lan). Find a synonym or word that has a similar meaning to "minimize."

    answer: p. 427. reduce; shrink.

174. *Nineteenth Century American Authors Match*

Match these titles with their authors.

Author		Title
____ 1.	Crane, Stephen	A *Eight Cousins*
____ 2.	London, Jack	*Little Women*
____ 3.	Harte, Bret	B *Pride and Prejudice*
____ 4.	Melville, Herman	C *The Wanderers*
____ 5.	Austen, Jane	*The Cat Who Went to*
____ 6.	Wallace, Lewis	*Heaven*

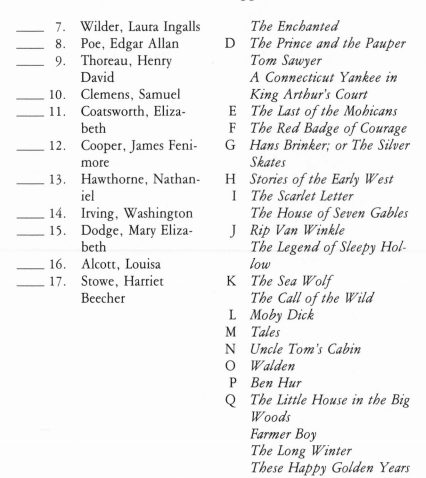

_____ 7. Wilder, Laura Ingalls

_____ 8. Poe, Edgar Allan

_____ 9. Thoreau, Henry David

_____ 10. Clemens, Samuel

_____ 11. Coatsworth, Elizabeth

_____ 12. Cooper, James Fenimore

_____ 13. Hawthorne, Nathaniel

_____ 14. Irving, Washington

_____ 15. Dodge, Mary Elizabeth

_____ 16. Alcott, Louisa

_____ 17. Stowe, Harriet Beecher

The Enchanted

D *The Prince and the Pauper*

Tom Sawyer

A Connecticut Yankee in King Arthur's Court

E *The Last of the Mohicans*

F *The Red Badge of Courage*

G *Hans Brinker; or The Silver Skates*

H *Stories of the Early West*

I *The Scarlet Letter*

The House of Seven Gables

J *Rip Van Winkle*

The Legend of Sleepy Hollow

K *The Sea Wolf*

The Call of the Wild

L *Moby Dick*

M *Tales*

N *Uncle Tom's Cabin*

O *Walden*

P *Ben Hur*

Q *The Little House in the Big Woods*

Farmer Boy

The Long Winter

These Happy Golden Years

ANSWERS

1:F.　2:K.　3:H.　4:L.　5:B.　6:P.　7:Q.　8:M.　9:O.
10:D.　11:C.　12:E.　13:I.　14:J.　15:G.　16:A.　17:N.

175. Famous Last Lines— Newbery Award Books

What is the title of the Newbery Award–winning fiction book from which the following last lines are taken:

1. "I cried for T.J. for T.J. and the land."
Roll of Thunder, Hear My Cry — Mildred Taylor

2. "Cusi and Chuto rose to face the east and to salute the Sun for a new beginning."
Secret of the Andes — Ann Nolan Clark

3. "And, in time, only the bards knew the truth of it."
High King — Lloyd Alexander

4. "Those two, who began in youth as master and slave, continued as companions in their maturity and ended as equals and as friends."
I, Juan de Pareja — Elizabeth Borton de Treviño

5. "There's a rumor going around that the beautiful girl arriving today might be the queen they've been waiting for."
Bridge to Terabithia — Katherine Paterson

6. "Julie pointed her boots toward Kapugen."
Julie of the Wolves — Jean Craighead George

7. "Using food for ballast I plan to spend one full year in the air, one year of truly delightful living, a year in a balloon!"
The Twenty-one Balloons — William Pène du Bois

8. "Years later, walking the earth as a man, it would all sweep back over him, again and again, like an echo on the wind."
Sounder — William Armstrong

9. "But they never learned what it was that Mrs. Whatsit, Mrs. Who, and Mrs. Which had to do, for there was a gust of wind, and they were gone."
A Wrinkle in Time — Madelaine L'Engle

10. "I would see once again as though they'd never ceased their dancing in my mind, black men and women and children lifting their tormented limbs in time to a reedy martial air, the dust rising from their joyless thumping, the sound of the fife finally drowned beneath the clanging of their chains."
The Slave Dancer — Paula Fox

11. "And his father's life, bullfighting, would stay a part of him, as it always had been, but in a different way than anyone had planned."
Shadow of a Bull — Maia Wojciechowska

12.   "It is for you and for me to write here our thoughts and tributes
to the King of the Wind and the slim brown horseboy who loved him."
      King of the Wind — Marguerite Henry

13.   "A man can stand up ..."
      Johnny Tremain — Esther Forbes

14.   "Dawn Boy was making way for the Bearer of the Day."
      Waterless Mountain — Laura Adams Armer

15.   "No one has claimed them yet."
      From the Mixed-Up Files of Mrs. Basil E. Frankweiler — E.L.
      Konigsburg

176. Famous First Lines—
Newbery Award Books

What is the title of the Newbery Award–winning fiction book
from which the following first lines are taken?

1.   "Sunday, October 17, 1830
          I, Catherine Cabot Hall, aged 13 years, 7 months, 8 days, of
Meredith in the State of New-Hampshire, do begin this book."
      *A Gathering of Days — A New England Girl's Journal, 1830–32
      A Novel* — Joan W. Blos

2.   "The sun sets in the west (just about everyone knows that), but
Sunset Towers faced east."
      The Westing Game — Ellen Raskin

3.   "I remember the day the Aleut ship came to our island."
      Island of the Blue Dolphins — Scott O'Dell

4.   "A boy stood on the path of the mountain overlooking the sea."
      The Bronze Bow — Elizabeth George Speare

5.   "My father is always talking about how a dog can be very educa-
tional for a boy."
      It's Like This, Cat — Emily Neville

6.   "I am Miguel."
      ...And Now Miguel — Joseph Krumgold

7. "Garnet, thought this must be the hottest day that had ever been in the world."
Thimble Summer—Elizabeth Enright

8. "Sara Godfrey was lying on the bed tying a kerchief on the dog, Boysie."
The Summer of the Swans—Betsy Byars

9. "Three children stood outside our gate in the bright October sunlight, silent and still as figurines in a gift shop window, watching each step I took as I came slowly down the flagstone walk across the lawn."
Up a Road Slowly—Irene Hunt

10. "On a morning in mid-April, 1687, the brigantine Dolphin left the open sea, sailed briskly across the sound to the wide mouth of the Connecticut River and into Saybrook harbor."
The Witch of Blackbird Pond—Elizabeth George Speare

11. "Mayo Cornelius Higgins raised his arms high to the sky and spread them wide."
M.C. Higgins, the Great—Virginia Hamilton

12. "The mules strained forward strongly, hoofs stomping, harness jingling."
Rifles for Watie—Harold Keith

13. "It was in the spring of the year 1241 that rumors began to travel along the highroad from Kiev in the land of Rus that the tartars of the East were again upon the march."
The Trumpeter of Krakow—Eric Kelly

14. "Up until I turned twelve years old the kind of friends I had were what you'd expect."
Onion John—Joseph Krumgold

15. "Mrs. Frisby, the head of a family of field mice, lived in an underground house in the vegetable garden of a farmer named Mr. Fitzgibbon."
Mrs. Frisby and the Rats of NIMH—Robert O'Brien

177. Card Catalog

Using the card catalog, locate the following.

1. Find a book about marine animals. Who is the author? What is the title of the book you found? (*Pick only one*; there may be several you find.) Who is the publisher? What is the copyright date? How many pages does it have? Are there illustrations? What is the call number?

2. What book did I.G. Edmonds write? Who is the publisher? What is the copyright date? Are there illustrations? What is one subject you can find this book under if you looked up the subject card? (*Pick only one; look at the bottom of the card.*) What is the call number?

3. Find a book on the topic The West-History. Who is the author? What is the title of the book? Who is the publisher? What is the copyright date? Are there illustrations? What is the call number?

4. Name *one* book that Emily Neville wrote. Are there illustrations? Who is the publisher? What is the copyright date? What is the call number? What are some other subjects one can find this book under?

5. Who wrote *The Arm of the Starfish*? What is the call number?

6. Who wrote *The Stonewalkers*? Is this a fiction (made-up story) or nonfiction (true) book?

7. Find a book on Mexico. (Pick only one nonfiction book.) What is the call number?

8. Find one book on babysitting. What is the call number? What is the title? Who wrote it? How many pages is it? Does it have illustrations?

9. Find one book on the topic "daughters—fiction." What is the call number? Who is the author? What is the latest copyright date? (The most recent date.) Is this a fiction or nonfiction book?

10. Who wrote *Sports Illustrated Backpacking*? What is the call number?

POSSIBLE ANSWERS

1. Boris Arnov, Jr. *Homes Beneath the Sea.* Little, Brown. 1969.

131p. photos. 574.5
    Ar

Elizabeth Clemons. *Tide Pools and Beaches.* Knopf. 1964. 79p. illus. 574.9
    Cl

Lou Jacobs. *Wonders of an Oceanarium; The Story of Marine Life in Captivity.* Golden Gate. 1965. 80p. photos. 574.92
    J

Edward Lindemann. *Water Animals for Your Microscope.* Crowell-Collier. 1967. 119p. illus. 574.92
    Li

John F. Waters. *Giant Sea Creatures; Real and Fantastic.* Follett. 1973. 128p. illus. and photos. 597.092
    W

2. *The Girls Who Talked to Ghosts: The Story of Katie and Margaretta Fox.* Holt. 1979. illustrated. Subjects: Jencken, Catherine Fox, 1836–1892; Fox, Margaret, 1833–1893; Spiritualists — Biography; Spiritualism — History.

3. *Cowboys and Cattle Country.* American Heritage. Amer. Her. 1961. 153p. illus. 978.5
    War

   Wounded Knee; An Indian History of the American West. Amy Ehrlich. Holt. 1974. illus. 202p. 970.5
    Eh

   Homesteaders and Indians. Dorothy Levenson. Watts. 1971. 90p. illus. map. 978
    L

4. *Fogarty.* Harper. 1969. 182p. no. illus. F no subject
    Nev

   It's Like This, Cat. Harper & Row. 1963. 180 p. illus. F
    Ne
cats — stories; New York (City) — Fiction

The Seventeenth-Street Gang. Harper & Row. 1966. illus. F
Ne

friendship-Fiction

5.   Madeleine L'Engle. F
          L'E

6.   Vivien Alcock. fiction

7.   *Mexico: Land of the Plumed Serpent.* 917.2
                                       G

Mexico. 917.2
Ha

Mexico; The Land and its People. 917.2
How

Mexico. 917.2
Joh

Land and People of Mexico. 917.2
La

Mexico. 972.08
Mex

Made in Mexico. 917.2
Ros

Hello, Mexico. 917.2
We

8.   649.1 *The Concise Guide to Baby-Sitting.* Rubie Saunders. 63p.
     S   illus.

9.   F Marilyn Sachs. *Fourteen.* 1985.
     Sac

10. Michael Sandi. 796.5
                San

178. *Library Skills Crossword I*

Across

1. This page is at the beginning of a book, and tells the name of each chapter.
2. A biography written by oneself.
3. Books created from a writer's imagination.
4. Tells one if a book contains old or recent information.
5. Where the story takes place.
6. The class number and author letter found on the spine of the book, and in the upper-left-hand corner of the catalog card.
7. The study of alphabets is found in this class.
8. What subject is 590?
9. What subject is 398?
10. What subject is 950?
11. A book of facts about numerous subjects in dictionary form.
12. The index in the *World Almanac* is found in the . . . of the book.

Down

1. This is an alphabetical listing of topics and words, and the page numbers at the end of a book.
2. Additional information at the end of a book.
3. An alphabetical listing of special words used in a book.
4. The index to the library's collection.
5. Books dealing with factual material.
6. Listings of books on a special subject.
7. One can find out where a particular desert is located with this dictionary.
8. What subject is 510?
9. What subject is 395?
10. 977.7 is . . . .
11. The number before the colon in the *Readers' Guide* is the . . . .
12. What subject is 780?

ANSWERS

Across

1. Table of contents

2. Autobiography
3. Fiction

Library Skills Crossword I

4.   Copyright
5.   Setting
6.   Call number
7.   Language
8.   Zoology
9.   Folklore
10. Asia
11. Encyclopedia
12. Front

Down

1.   Index

2.   Appendix
3.   Glossary
4.   Card catalog
5.   Nonfiction
6.   Bibliographies
7.   Geographical
8.   Math
9.   Etiquette
10. Iowa
11. Volume
12. Music

179. *Library Skills Crossword II*

Name the topics for the corresponding Dewey Decimal numbers.

Across

1.   391.5
2.   678.2
3.   741
4.   948.1
5.   963
6.   620.182
7.   629.4
8.   523.7
9.   523.8
10. 690
11. 793.3
12. 792
13. 371
14. 915

Down

1.   391.7
2.   613
3.   595.1
4.   297
5.   624.2
6.   821
7.   961.2
8.   495.1
9.   596
10. 795.4
11. 549
12. 374
13. 160
14. 133.4
15. 332.4
16. 391
17. 934

Library Skills Crossword II

ANSWERS

Across		Down	
1.	Hair styles	1.	Jewelry
2.	Rubber	2.	Hygiene
3.	Drawing	3.	Worms
4.	Norway	4.	Islam
5.	Ethiopia	5.	Bridges
6.	Copper	6.	English poetry
7.	Astronautics	7.	Libya
8.	Sun	8.	Chinese (Language)
9.	Stars	9.	Chordata (Vertebrates)
10.	Buildings	10.	Card games
11.	Dancing	11.	Mineralogy
12.	Theater	12.	Adult education
13.	School	13.	Logic
14.	Asia	14.	Witchcraft
		15.	Money
		16.	Fashion
		17.	India

V. REFERENCE BOOKS

180. Reference Sources

Locate 3 to 5 examples of each of the following types of reference books in the school library media center:

1. **Bibliographies**: descriptive, systematic lists of books. They are guides to the literature of a particular field, either general or specific in nature.

2. **Indexes & Abstracts**: systematic listings that trace and identify materials. An abstract is a summary of an article or other piece of writing.

3. **Encyclopedias, General**: volumes containing informational articles on subjects in every area of knowledge. Arranged in alphabetical order. Used to answer specific questions about a specific topic or person, or a general query such as, "I want some information about dogs."

4. **Special Subject Encyclopedias**: used to explore in depth a specific area or subject of interest. These are sources of background information.

5. **Special Subject Dictionaries**: used to look up definitions in a specific area or subject of interest. They deal with all aspects of words from proper definitions to spelling. Some types of dictionaries are: historical; biographical; slang; abbreviations; foreign language; thesaurus; subject.

6. **Quotations**: give famous quotes from famous people, and the source.

7. **Almanacs**: compendiums of useful statistics and data. They give information about personalities, countries, subjects, events, etc. Very general in nature.

8. **Special Subject Almanacs**: compendiums as above, but limited to a particular subject. Sometimes called annuals or yearbooks. Some are quite broad in scope.

9. **Yearbook** or **Annual**: an annual compendium of statistics and data for that one year.

10. **Directories**: lists of organizations or persons, systematically arranged, usually in a classed or alphabetical order. They give addresses, affiliations, and other information for individuals, and addresses, functions, officers, etc., for organizations.

11. **Handbooks** and **Manuals**: although these are similar, a handbook is usually a group of facts centered around one main theme or subject area, while a manual is more equated with how-to-do-it, whether it be fixing a flat tire or cooking a meal.

12. **Biographical Sources**: books about famous people or people distinguished in a particular field of interest.

13. **Geographical Sources**: books which contain maps and information about countries. These include atlases, which not only contain maps, but may illustrate themes such as historical development, social development, and scientific centers. These also include gazetteers, dictionaries of place names, and guidebooks. A gazetteer is a geographical dictionary, more comprehensive than the atlas. Guide books are limited to one specific area, city, town, county, state, or nation, and point to the highlights of travel.

14. **Statistical Reference Sources**: include the classification, collection, interpretation and analysis of various numerical facts or data.

15. **Government Documents**: official publications ordered and published by the federal, state, or local government.

181. *Abridged Readers' Guide to Periodical Literature*

1. Find an article in the *Abridged Readers' Guide* on rock music. What is the title of the article? Who wrote the article? In what magazine can you find this article? On what pages? What is the date of the magazine? Are there illustrations? Are there other related topics or "See Also" subjects you can find under rock music?

2. Find an article about George Bush. What is the title of the

article? Who wrote the article? In what magazine can you find this article? On what pages? What is the date of the magazine? Are there illustrations? Are there other related topics or "See Also" subjects you can find under George Bush?

3. Find an article about drug abuse. Are there other related topics you can find under the "See Also"? What is the title of the article? Who wrote the article? In what magazine can you find this article? On what pages? What is the date of the magazine? Are there illustrations?

4. Find an article about softball. Are there other related topics you can find under the "See Also"? What is the title of the article? Who wrote the article? In what magazine can you find this article? On what pages? What is the date of the magazine? Are there illustrations?

5. Find an article about dating ("Social Customs"). Are there other related topics you can find under the "See Also"? What is the title of the article? Who wrote the article? In what magazine can you find this article? On what pages? What is the date of the magazine? Are there illustrations?

6. Find an article on "Cooking, French." What is the title of the article? Who wrote the article? In what magazine can you find this article? On what pages? What is the date of the magazine? Are there illustrations? Are there other related topics or "See Also" subjects you can find?

7. Find an article on pets. Are there other related topics you can find under the "See Also"? What is the title of the article? Who wrote the article? In what magazine can you find this article? On what pages? What is the date of the magazine? Are there illustrations?

8. Find an article on space stations. What is the title of the article? Who wrote the article? In what magazine can you find this article? On what pages? What is the date of the magazine? Are there illustrations? Are there other related topics or "See Also" subjects you can find under space stations?

9. Find an article on nuclear industry. Are there other related topics you can find under the "See Also"? What is the title of the article? Who wrote the article? In what magazine can you find this article? On what pages? What is the date of the magazine? Are there illustrations?

10. Find an article on Antarctic research. What is the title of the article? Who wrote the article? In what magazine can you find this

article? On what pages? What is the date of the magazine? Are there illustrations? Are there other related topics or "See Also" subjects you can find under Antarctica?

182. Webster's Biographical Dictionary

Using *Webster's Biographical Dictionary,* answer the following:

1. Who was James Cook known as? (Captain Cook)
2. Who was Percy H. Fitzgerald? (Irish sculptor and writer)
3. Who was Montezuma? (name of two Aztec rulers)
4. Who was Vanderbilt? (name of an American family prominent in transportation and finance)
5. Who was Sir George Grove? (English engineer and writer on music)
6. Who was Thomas Boston? (Scottish Presbyterian clergyman)
7. Who was John Donne? (English poet)
8. Who was Carl Haag? (German-born British painter)
9. Who was Joachim Murat? (French cavalry commander)
10. Who was Rivington? (name of a family of English publishers)
11. Who was Riza Shah Pahlavi? (King of Iran)
12. Who was Lars Fredrik Nilson? (Swedish physicist)
13. Who was Alfred B. Nobel? (Swedish manufacturer, inventor, and philanthropist)
14. Who was Sir Lionel Halsey? (British naval officer)
15. Who was John Fitch? (American inventor)

183. Food—Webster's Geographical Dictionary

Match the physical places that sound like food to the correct description found in *Webster's Geographical Dictionary:*

____ 1.	a borough in England.	A.	Milk
____ 2.	islands off East Indonesia.	B.	Lemon Rock
		C.	Onion
____ 3.	a county in Georgia.	D.	Frankfurt
____ 4.	a city in Arkansas.	E.	Appleby
____ 5.	a dam in New York.	F.	Mango
____ 6.	a river in Maine and New Hampshire.	G.	Orange Walk
		H.	Pea Ridge
____ 7.	three small islands off coast of Ireland called Skelligs.	I.	Spice Islands
		J.	Corn Islands
		K.	Raisin River
		L.	Basilan
____ 8.	a river in Michigan.	M.	Salmon Falls
____ 9.	former district in British Honduras.	N.	Peach
		O.	Olive Bridge Dam
____ 10.	a city in Arkansas.	P.	Hamburg
____ 11.	government district in Germany.	Q.	Salt Island
		R.	Pepperell
____ 12.	district in Scotland.	S.	Breadalbane
____ 13.	a river in Montana and Canada.	T.	Egg Island
____ 14.	town in Massachusetts.		
____ 15.	one of the British Virgin Islands, West Indies.		
____ 16.	island group off Philippines.		
____ 17.	one of the Fiji Islands.		
____ 18.	barren rock off Hawaii.		
____ 19.	two small islands in Caribbean Sea.		
____ 20.	a river in Vermont.		

ANSWERS

1:E.   2:I.   3:N.   4:P or H.   5:O.   6:M.   7:B.   8:K.   9:G.

10:H or P.   11:D.   12:S.   13:A.   14:R.   15:Q.   16:L.   17:F.
18:T.   19:J.   20:C.

184. Animals—Webster's Geographical Dictionary

Match the physical places that sound like an animal to the correct description found in *Webster's Geographical Dictionary:*

_____ 1. a river in Ohio.
_____ 2. an island in the At-
           lantic Ocean off
           Florida.
_____ 3. a small river in En-
           gland.
_____ 4. a peak in New
           Mexico.
_____ 5. a city in ancient
           Numidia, Algeria.
_____ 6. a peak in Montana.
_____ 7. a river in Wiscon-
           sin.
_____ 8. one of the Japanese
           Islands.
_____ 9. inlet of the Atlantic
           Ocean off Africa.
_____ 10. a river in Mississippi
           and Tennessee.
_____ 11. a peak in Oregon.
_____ 12. an island off Aus-
           tralia.
_____ 13. an island off Florida.
_____ 14. a creek in Nebraska.
_____ 15. inlet of the Mediter-
           ranean Sea off
           coast of France.
_____ 16. a small island off

A. Grouse Mountain
B. Tiger Bay
C. Dog Island
D. Bear
E. Kangaroo Island
F. Deer Creek
G. Snake Creek
H. Fox River
I. Moose Lake
J. Gulf of Lions
K. Hippo Regius
L. Dove
M. Fishers Island
N. Yaku
O. Pelican Island
P. Owl Creek
Q. Goat Mountain
R. Skunk River
S. Sheep Rock
T. Wolf River

coast of Connecti-
cut.
_____ 17. a river in Iowa.
_____ 18. a creek in South
          Dakota.
_____ 19. a lake in Canada.
_____ 20. a river in Idaho and
          Utah.

ANSWERS

1:F.   2:O.   3:L.   4:A.   5:K.   6:Q.   7:H.   8:N.   9:B.
10:T.   11:S.   12:E.   13:C.   14:G.   15:J.   16:M.   17:R.   18:P.
19:I.   20:D.

185. Color—Webster's Geographical Dictionary

Match the physical places that sound like a color to the correct
description found in *Webster's Geographical Dictionary*:

_____ 1.	a river in South In-diana.	A.	Maroon Peak
		B.	Gold Beach
_____ 2.	a river in Louisiana.	C.	Orange
_____ 3.	counties in nine states of the U.S.	D.	Gray
		E.	Pearl
_____ 4.	Name of three rivers of the U.S.	F.	Black
		G.	Tana
_____ 5.	counties in eight states of the U.S.	H.	Ruby Lake
		I.	Yellow River
_____ 6.	Defile east of the Presidential Range, White Mountains, New Hampshire.	J.	Blue
		K.	Silver City
		L.	Red
		M.	Emerald Isle
_____ 7.	Name of several rivers in U.S.	N.	Pinkham Notch
		O.	Rose Peak
_____ 8.	a river in northern Illinois.	P.	Salmon River Mountains
		Q.	Green

_____ 9.   a river in Arkansas.   R.   Peach Tree
_____ 10. a river in East   S.   White
           Africa.   T.   Brown
_____ 11. a creek in Georgia.
_____ 12. name of counties in
           two states of the
           U.S.
_____ 13. a mountain in Colo-
           rado.
_____ 14. cluster of mountain
           ranges in Idaho.
_____ 15. a ghost town in
           Idaho.
_____ 16. on the corner of
           Oregon on Pacific
           Ocean.
_____ 17. a lake in Nevada.
_____ 18. Ireland.
_____ 19. a mountain in
           Arizona.
_____ 20. a river in Missis-
           sippi.

ANSWERS

1:J.   2:F.   3:T.   4:L.   5:C.   6:N.   7:I.   8:Q.   9:S.   10:G.
11:R.   12:D.   13:A.   14:P.   15:K.   16:B.   17:H.   18:M.   19:O.
20:E.

186. Constellations

Using the *World Almanac*, name the constellation:

1.   that sounds like a book called *The Andromeda Strain* by M. Crichton, and means chained maiden? (Andromeda)
2.   that sounds like one of the manned spacecraft, is the third sign of the zodiac, and means twins? (Gemini)
3.   that sounds like an illness, and means a crab? (Cancer)
4.   that sounds like a member of the cat family, and means lynx? (Lynx)

5. that sounds like a boy's first name, and means a lion? (Leo)

6. that sounds like a depression shaped like a bowl, and means cup? (Crater)

7. that sounds like a girl's first name, and means a square rule? (Norma)

8. that sounds like an artist who creates statues or shapes? (Sculptor)

9. that means a flying horse? (Pegasus)

10. that means a dove? (Columba)

11. that means fishes? (Pisces)

12. that means queen? (Cassiopeia)

13. that means hunter? (Orion)

14. that means archer? (Sagittarius)

15. that means peacock? (Pavo)

187. Peaks

Using the *World Almanac,* find the peak or mountain that reminds you of:

1. the 25th President of the United States? (McKinley)

2. the last name of the inventor of the cotton gin? (Whitney)

3. a type of bear? (Grizzly)

4. the opposite of moonlight? (Sunlight)

5. a famous English war leader during World War II (Churchill)

6. a royal leader of a country? (King)

7. an airport in Boston, Mass.? (Logan)

8. a boy's first name that begins with "r"? (Russell)

9. a boy's first name that begins with "k"? (Keith)

10. an Ivy League university in New Haven? (Yale)

11. the home of a king? (Castle)

12. the 16th president of the United States? (Lincoln)

13. a famous United States World War II general? (MacArthur)

14. a sportsman looking for deer? (Hunter)

15. a dark red color? (Maroon)

16. a member of the Iroquoian people? (Huron)
17. the center of our government? (Capitol)
18. what they have in Egypt? (Pyramid)
19. the 35th president of the United States? (Kennedy)
20. the anonym of diminutive? (Massive)

188. Names—Webster's Geographical Dictionary

Using *Webster's Geographical Dictionary*, match the following places that sound like first names:

___ 1.	Ava	A	a chain of shoals about 30 miles long between Ceylon and SE coast of India
___ 2.	Anthony		
___ 3.	Ambrose Channel		
___ 4.	Allen		
___ 5.	Adam's Bridge	B	a county in New Brunswick, Canada
___ 6.	Alessandria		
___ 7.	Amber	C	counties in Illinois and North Carolina
___ 8.	Alexander		
___ 9.	Arnold	D	channel across Sandy Hook Bar, entrance to New York Harbor
___ 10.	Alberta		
___ 11.	Allison		
___ 12.	Arthur	E	a city in SE Texas
___ 13.	Alfred	F	a town in SW Maine
___ 14.	Andrew	G	a province of Italy
___ 15.	Alice	H	a city in S. Missouri
___ 16.	Anna	I	a town in SW Quebec, Canada
___ 17.	Alexandria		
___ 18.	Alma	J	a ruined ancient city in NW India
___ 19.	Albina		
___ 20.	Alta	K	a city in S. Texas
___ 21.	Amelia	L	a city in SE Michigan
___ 22.	Albert	M	a river in N. Norway
___ 23.	Adrian	N	a city in S. Kansas
___ 24.	Amos	O	a county in Virginia
___ 25.	Alvin	P	a parish in Louisiana

Q   a seaport town in NE
    Surinam
R   a city in SW Pennsylvania
S   a county in Missouri
T   a city in SE Georgia
U   a province in W. Canada
V   a county in Nebraska
W   a city in SW Illinois
X   a city in central Indiana
Y   a town in NE central Iowa

ANSWERS

1:H.   2:N.   3:D.   4:P.   5:A.   6:G.   7:J.   8:C.   9:R.
10:U.   11:Y.   12:V.   13:F.   14:S.   15:K.   16:W.   17:X.   18:T.
19:Q.   20:M.   21:O.   22:B.   23:L.   24:I.   25:E.

189. *Webster's Geographical Dictionary*

Using *Webster's Geographical Dictionary* answer the following:

1. What and where is "Azogue"? (Quicksilver mines known to Romans and Moors, also producing lead and sulfur. P. 30.)

2. What and where is "LeeLanau"? (A county in Michigan. P. 603.)

3. What are the "Palisades"? (A line of high cliffs of traprock about 15 miles long on the west bank of the Hudson River in southeast New York and northeast New Jersey. P. 847.)

4. How high is Mount Le Conte in California? (13,960 ft. P. 602.)

5. What are the chief islands of the "Leeward Islands" group? (Huahine, Raiatea, and Tahaa. P. 603.)

6. What was "Blumenthal"? (A former commune in Germany. P. 139.)

7. Of what type of rock is "Independence Rock"? (Granite. P. 487.)

8. Of how many islands are the "Scilly Isles" comprised? (140 small islands. P. 1017.)

9. What is the "Vaucluse"? (A department of France. P. 1207.)
10. Where is "Coburg"? (Southeast Australia. P. 244.)

190. Body Parts—Webster's Geographical Dictionary

Find as many place names as you can in the *Webster's Geographical Dictionary* that sound like a part of the human body, and match them to their correct places.

____	1. Lungchow	A.	river in North Dakota.
____	2. Toe Head	B.	peninsula off coast of Scotland.
____	3. Bone		
____	4. Palm Beach	C.	a group of lakes in Western New York.
____	5. Hipswell		
____	6. Heart	D.	a cape off of coast of Scotland.
____	7. Eye		
____	8. Leghorn	E.	a city in Alabama.
____	9. Braintree	F.	an islet of the Leeward Islands in Hawaii.
____	10. Headland		
____	11. Jawor	G.	a city in Kansas.
____	12. Footscray	H.	seaport commune in Italy.
____	13. Necker	I.	manufacturing city in South Victoria, Australia.
____	14. Finger Lakes		
____	15. Bilecik	J.	this name was given by U.S. Marines to the Umurbrogol Mt. on Peleliu Island in the Pacific.
____	16. Cheektowaga		
____	17. Bloody Nose Ridge		
____	18. Arma		
____	19. Muscle Shoals	K.	town and port in China.
____	20. Rib Mountain	L.	rapids in the Tennessee River in Alabama.
____	21. Colon		
____	22. Chester	M.	town in Massachusetts.
____	23. Backbone Mountain	N.	vilayet in Turkey.
____	24. Back River	O.	commune and seaport in Algeria.
____	25. Elbow Lake		

____ 26. Liverpool

____ 27. Hand

P. unincorportated urban community in New York.

Q. village in Yorkshire, England.

R. city in Poland.

S. the highest point in the state of Wisconsin.

T. a county in Florida.

U. a county in South Dakota.

V. town in Argentina.

W. a village in Minnesota.

X. the highest point in Maryland.

Y. a river in Canada; was called Great Fish River.

Z. town in Connecticut.

AA a city in England.

ANSWERS

1:K.   2:D.   3:O.   4:T.   5:Q.   6:A.   7:B.   8:H.   9:M.
10:E.   11:R.   12:I.   13:F.   14:C.   15:N.   16:P.   17:J.   18:G.
19:L.   20:S.   21:V.   22:Z.   23:X.   24:Y.   25:W.   26:AA.
27:U.

191. Bird Match

Match the state with the state bird, using an encyclopedia:

____ 1. Connecticut

____ 2. Florida

____ 3. Ohio

____ 4. New York

____ 5. Utah

____ 6. Massachusetts

____ 7. Georgia

A. chickadee

B. cactus wren

C. roadrunner

D. ruffed grouse

E. mockingbird

F. hermit thrush

G. common loon

_____ 8.	Delaware	H.	lark bunting
_____ 9.	Maryland	I.	brown thrasher
_____ 10.	Arizona	J.	bluebird
_____ 11.	Alabama	K.	brown pelican
_____ 12.	New Mexico	L.	purple finch
_____ 13.	North Dakota	M.	robin
_____ 14.	Pennsylvania	N.	yellow-hammer
_____ 15.	Vermont	O.	willow goldfinch
_____ 16.	Colorado	P.	blue henchicken
_____ 17.	New Hampshire	Q.	cardinal
_____ 18.	Minnesota	R.	western meadowlark
_____ 19.	Louisiana	S.	sea gull
_____ 20.	Washington	T.	Baltimore oriole

ANSWERS

1:M.   2:E.   3:Q.   4:J.   5:S.   6:A.   7:I.   8:P.   9:T.   10:B.
11:N.   12:C.   13:R.   14:D.   15:F.   16:H.   17:L.   18:G.   19:K.
20:O.

VI. FICTION CROSSWORD PUZZLES

192. *Ginger Pye (by Eleanor Estes)*

Across

1. Setting of the book.
2. Ginger is a . . . .
3. The clue.
4. Ginger . . . ?
5. Rachel reads *The Secret*. . . .
6. The uncle.
7. The uncle's age.
8. How they obtain Ginger.
9. Gracie is a . . . present to Mama.
10. Rachel's best friend.
11. The steamboat . . . Peck.
12. Reverend . . . .
13. Sam had a job there.
14. The Moffats live near this place.

Down

1. Wedding present to the mother.
2. Family's last name.
3. Father is a famous . . . man.
4. The spinster auntie.
5. Mr. Pye is called there for work.
6. The cat's age.

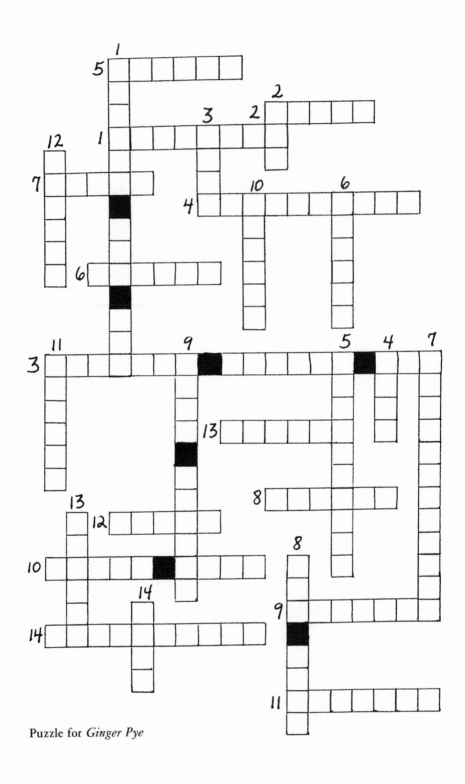

Puzzle for *Ginger Pye*

7. What day Ginger disappears.
8. Gracie is known as the . . . cat.
9. Jared's best friend.
10. They wanted a puppy from his barn.
11. How long it took to find Ginger.
12. A birthday party.
13. A famous cave.
14. "Dusting the . . . ."

ANSWERS

Across

1. Cranbury
2. Puppy
3. Mustard yellow hat
4. Disappears
5. Garden
6. Bennie
7. Three
8. Bought
9. Wedding
10. Addie Egan
11. Richard
12. Gandy
13. Church
14. Ashbellows

Down

1. Gracie the cat
2. Pye
3. Bird
4. Hoyt
5. Washington
6. Eleven
7. Thanksgiving
8. New York
9. Dick Badger
10. Speedy
11. Months
12. Stokes
13. Judges
14. Pews

193. *The High King (by Lloyd Alexander)*

Across

1. This is the finale to the chronicles of . . . .
2. The death-lord.
3. The prince, with Taran, who raises an army against Arawn.
4. A battle on an . . . scale.
5. The crow.

6. Taran's stallion.
7. The stronghold of Queen Achren.
8. Taran's companion.
9. Land of the dead.
10. "The King of . . . ."
11. What Taran wears on his shoulder.
12. What marches against Arawn?
13. "The river of . . . ."

Down

1. The assistant pig-keeper.
2. The sword.
3. The princess.
4. Arawn's stronghold.
5. Ancient enchanter.
6. Grandson of Rhydderch.
7. What happens to Lord Gwydion?
8. The sneering scoundrel.
9. Small-hearted giant.
10. Consort to Arawn.
11. "King . . . castle."
12. The winter . . . .
13. Battle of good and . . . .

ANSWERS

Across

1. Prydain
2. Arawn
3. Gwydion
4. Epic
5. Kaw
6. Melynlas
7. Spiral castle
8. Llyr
9. Annuvin
10. Mona
11. Battle horn
12. Army
13. Eggs

Down

1. Taran
2. Drnwyn
3. Eilonwy
4. Annuvin
5. Dallben
6. Rhitta
7. Slain
8. Magg
9. Glew
10. Achren
11. Smoit's
12. March
13. Evil

Puzzle for *The High King*

194. It's Like This, Cat (by Emily Neville)

Across

1. Calls Kate the . . . .
2. The janitor.
3. The local paper, . . . and . . . .

Puzzle for *It's Like This, Cat*

4. The local paper, ... and ....
5. He has one in his hair.
6. His friend, last name.
7. A park.
8. Fulton's.
9. Dave's hair coloring.
10. A place in Jersey.
11. The friends do this together.
12. The hospital.
13. Kate's surname.

Down

1. One of Kate's cats.
2. What does the hero "adopt"?
3. What was taken from the cellar?
4. Setting.
5. Dave's first friendship with one.
6. Dave begins to understand him.
7. What is played in the street?
8. The Jewish New Year.
9. They do this together.
10. Tom's parents live there.
11. Expedition by ....

ANSWERS

Across

1. Cat woman
2. Butch
3. Town village
4. Cowlick
5. Ransom
6. Joey
7. Gramercy
8. Fish market
9. Sandy
10. Palisades
11. Bike
12. Speyer
13. Carmichael

Down

1. Susan
2. Tomcat
3. Suitcase
4. New York City
5. Girl

6. Father
7. Stickball
8. Rosh Hashanah
9. Rollerskate
10. Mid-west
11. Ferry

195. *Julie of the Wolves*
(by Jean Craighead George)

Across

1. Julie is the adopted daughter of . . . .
2. The light summer woman's dress.
3. In what sea was her father lost?
4. Julie is accepted in a pack.
5. Julie finds her home situation . . . .
6. The view in every direction.
7. Julie is without . . . .
8. The wolf is Miyax's adopted . . . .
9. Julie lures these animals to her.
10. Julie has no direction-finder.
11. A woman's knife.
12. A bold sea bird.
13. An island.
14. What holds the spirits of the animals?
15. Who asked her if she wanted a pen pal?
16. What grade is Amy in?
17. Her knife is shaped like a half . . . .
18. Julie walked to school last winter.
19. One of the other wolves.
20. Another wolf.
21. Another wolf.
22. Another color of the Bladder Feast.

Down

1. What is her parka made of?
2. What does the woflr fight?
3. Where did the family used to live?
4. She is traveling on this slope.
5. The book is about . . . .
6. 800 miles from this range to the Beaufort Sea.
7. A bird.
8. Describes the slope to the Arctic Ocean.
9. Julie's future will never be . . . .
10. The wolves are like her . . . .
11. She builds a house of this material.
12. Her father had been the manager of a herd.
13. This subject comes easily to Julie.
14. This subject also comes easily to her.
15. Daylight.
16. Celebration of the Bladder . . . .
17. A wolf.
18. We see the Eskimos' way of life.
19. These animals are seen.
20. One of the colors of the Bladder Feast.
21. A color of the Bladder Feast.
22. Zit . . . a wolf.

ANSWERS

Across

1. Martha
2. Kuspuck
3. Bering
4. Wolves
5. Intolerable
6. Same
7. Food
8. Father
9. Squirrels
10. Compass
11. Ulo
12. Jaeger
13. Nunivak
14. Bladders
15. Pollock
16. Eighth
17. Moon
18. Barrow
19. Silver
20. Sister
21. Jello
22. Blue

Puzzle for *Julie of the Wolves*

Down

1. Sealskin
2. Caribou
3. Mekoryuk
4. North
5. Survival
6. Chukchi
7. Tornait
8. Barren
9. Easy
10. Brothers
11. Sod
12. Reindeer
13. Math
14. English
15. Quag
16. Feast
17. Nails
18. Rituals
19. Lemmings
20. Fire red
21. Black
22. Was

196. *The Summer of the Swans (by Betsy Byars)*

Across

1. Heroine.
2. Her retarded brother.
3. Who does the heroine dislike?
4. One of the searchers for the brother.
5. The English teacher.
6. Heroine compares her summer to a . . . .
7. What does her brother like to listen to?
8. Setting.
9. On what do they go for a ride?
10. A story of summer days.
11. Sara wears sneakers.
12. Sara's best dress.
13. The . . . house.
14. The outcome of the search.

ANSWERS

Across

1. Sara Godfrey
2. Charlie
3. Joe Melby
4. Rhodes
5. Marshall

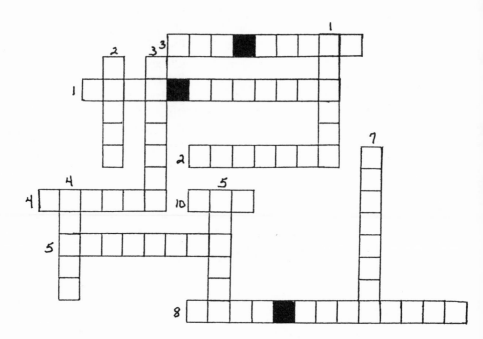

Puzzle for *The Summer of the Swans*

Down

1. Their dog.
2. A sister.
3. The drugstore.
4. The principal of the school.
5. Her aunt ... Weicek.
6. What do they watch at the lake?
7. The book is about slow ... children.
8. What happens to her brother?
9. Sara cannot explain her inner feelings.
10. The ... house.
11. Sara wears the same size shoe as .....
12. Willie's last name.

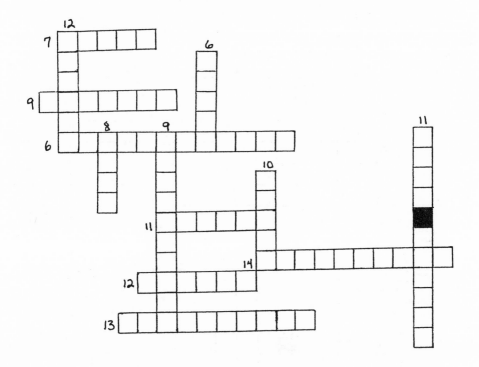

Puzzle for *The Summer of the Swans*

ANSWERS

6. Kaleidoscope
7. Watch
8. West Virginia
9. Scooter
10. Two
11. Orange
12. Jersey
13. Hutchinson
14. Successful

Down

1. Boysie
2. Wanda

3. Carter's
4. Homer
5. Willie
6. Swans
7. Learning
8. Lost
9. Discontent
10. Akers
11. Bull Durham
12. Weicek

Puzzle for *Village of the Vampire Cat*

197. *Village of the Vampire Cat (by Lensey Namioka)*

Across

1. What country does this book take place in?
2. One samurai.
3. An unemployed samurai.
4. The village carpenter.
5. The village carpenter's daughter.
6. The tea ceremony master's son.
7. Asa's dog.
8. This is a story of . . . .
9. The story of . . . fiction.
10. The village is terrorized by a . . . .
11. What does the cat try to seize?
12. Who does the cat try to kill, Ikken's . . . ?
13. Who does the village fear?
14. The killings are . . . .
15. Who helps the two samurai fight the cat?

Down

1. Holiday.
2. The second samurai.
3. A tea ceremony master.
4. Widow of the tea ceremony master.
5. The widow's daughter.
6. The leader of an outlaw band.
7. A merchant.
8. This is a story of . . . .
9. A character in the book.
10. Another character in the book, . . . keeper.
11. In what art is Zenta and Matsuzo trained?
12. The sound of the cat.
13. The cat is shrouded in?
14. Era in history.
15. The killings are almost . . . .

ANSWERS

Across

1. Japan
2. Zenta
3. Ronin
4. Jiro
5. Kiku
6. Shunken
7. Kongomaru
8. Adventure
9. Samurai
10. Killer
11. Inheritance
12. Niece
13. Extortionists
14. Brutal
15. Villagers

Down

1. New Year's
2. Matsuzo
3. Ikken
4. Toshi
5. Asa
6. Ryutaro
7. Hirobei
8. Terror
9. Exorcist
10. Tavern
11. Martial
12. Mewing
13. Black
14. Feudal
15. Supernatural

198. A Wrinkle in Time (by Madeleine L'Engle)

Across

1. A wrinkle in time is a . . . .
2. Adventures in . . . .
3. A popular boy.
4. Meg's father.
5. The kind of work her father does.
6. Mrs. . . . .
7. A twin brother.
8. The big black dog.
9. The constable's wife.
10. Heroine's mother's hair.
11. The dog is part . . . .
12. "The man with red . . . ."
13. Her mother has a degree in . . . .
14. Times is the fourth . . . .

Puzzle for *A Wrinkle in Time*

130 More Books Appeal

15. She sees her father here.
16. The second sign of returning consciousness.

Down

1. Genre of book.
2. Adventures in . . . .
3. Heroine's informal name.
4. Baby brother.
5. Who they are searching for.
6. Her father works for them.
7. Book considers problem of good and . . . .
8. A twin brother.
9. Heroine's formal name.
10. How many sheets were stolen?
11. Heroine's mother's eyes.
12. Imports and exports.
13. The dog is also part . . . .
14. Father's exact line of work.
15. Her mother has a degree in . . . .
16. The first sign of returning consciousness.

ANSWERS

Across

1. Tesseract
2. Space
3. Calvin O'Keefe
4. Scientist
5. Secret
6. Whatsit
7. Dennis
8. Fortinbras
9. Buncombe
10. Red
11. Greyhound
12. Eyes
13. Bacteriology
14. Dimension
15. Cell
16. Sound

Down

1. Science fiction
2. Time
3. Meg
4. Charles Wallace
5. Father
6. Government
7. Evil
8. Sandy
9. Margaret Murry
10. Twelve
11. Violet
12. Nicaragua
13. Setter
14. Physicist
15. Biology
16. Cold

199. *Bridge to Terabithia (by Katherine Paterson)*

Across

1. The hideaway.
2. Jess wants to be the fastest . . . .
3. The elementary school.
4. One theme.
5. Hero's hobby.
6. The fifth grade teacher.
7. Leslie's parents were . . . .
8. Hero's father goes there.
9. The grade at school.
10. Where is Leslie sent?
11. The boys enjoyed watching them on TV.
12. The weather during the accident.
13. Hero's father does this.

Down

1. Setting.
2. The 10-year-old boy.
3. One theme.
4. Leslie's hobby.
5. Music teacher, Miss . . . .
6. Leslie's last name.
7. The "real giant's" friend.
8. What happens to Leslie?
9. Hero writes a composition.
10. Mr. Burke was repairing an old house.
11. Hero is taught that this is nothing to be ashamed of.

ANSWERS

Across

1. Terabithia
2. Runner
3. Lark Creek
4. Friendship
5. Draw
6. Myers
7. Writers
8. Washington
9. Fifth

Puzzle for *Bridge to Terabithia*

ANSWERS

Across

10. Pennsylvania
11. Redskins
12. Storm
13. Haul

Down

1. Virginia
2. Jesse Oliver Aarons

3. Death
4. Scuba diving
5. Edmunds
6. Burke
7. Wilma
8. Dies
9. Football
10. Perkins
11. Love

200. From the Mixed-Up Files of Mrs. Basil E. Frankweiler (by E.L. Konigsburg)

Across

1. The museum.
2. The former owner of the statue.
3. The former owner of the statue's lawyer.
4. The scene of an alleged murder.
5. One of her problems is she felt . . . .
6. Her mother's club.
7. One thing they gave up to save . . . sundaes.
8. Jamie has one.
9. The day they plan to go.
10. The school bus driver.
11. Heroine's grade level.
12. A guard at the Metropolitan.
13. The statue was gotten from a dealer there.
14. What are they looking for on the statue?
15. What is at the bottom of the statue?
16. Who they see.

Puzzle for *From the Mixed-Up Files of Mrs. Basil E. Frankweiler*

Down

1. The heroine is a good . . . .
2. Jamie and Buddy play . . . .
3. The public relations man at the museum.
4. Her brother had some.
5. Heroine is almost . . . years old.
6. They get the train there.
7. A boy in her class.
8. Claudia plays it.
9. What Jamie does.
10. The road traveled.
11. What happened to Dudley's wife?
12. The country estate is located in . . . .
13. The statue is how many inches?
14. Egyptian tombs.

ANSWERS

Across		Down	
1.	Metropolitan	1.	Organizer
2.	Frankweiler	2.	Cards
3.	Saxonberg	3.	Lowery
4.	Bed	4.	Money
5.	Same	5.	Twelve
6.	Mah-Jong	6.	Greenwich
7.	Hot fudge	7.	Johnathan
8.	Transistor radio	8.	Violin
9.	Wednesday	9.	Gambles
10.	Herbert	10.	Boston Post
11.	Sixth	11.	Murdered
12.	Morris	12.	Farmington
13.	Bologna	13.	Twenty-four
14.	Fingerprints	14.	Mastaba
15.	Mark		
16.	Class		

201. *Jacob Have I Loved*
(by Katherine Paterson)

Across

1. The men of the island work as . . . .
2. A little ditch of water and a natural garbage dump.
3. One type of catch.
4. The father.
5. One of Captain Billy's sons.
6. Where is the name on each boat?
7. The general store.
8. Most of the island is saltwater . . . .
9. The teacher's girlfriend lives in what city?
10. Where do they get their mother?
11. Louise feels . . . .

Down

1. The high school teacher.
2. The father's boat.
3. What does the mother do?
4. One type of catch.
5. Type of crabs.
6. One of Captain Billy's sons.
7. Family's last name.
8. Type of bushes found on the island.
9. Type of grass.
10. Name of friend.
11. The mother belongs to this church.
12. The store is painted . . . .
13. Caroline is forever being . . . .

ANSWERS

Across

1. Watermen
2. South Gut
3. Peelers
4. Joseph
5. Richard
6. Stern
7. Kellam

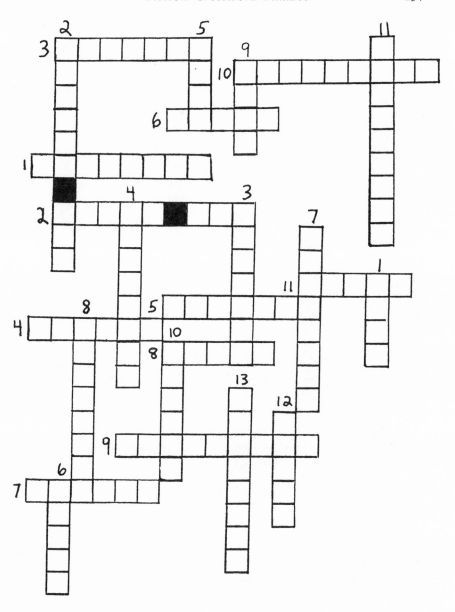

Puzzle for *Jacob Have I Loved*

8. Marsh
9. Baltimore
10. Crisfield
11. Angry

Down

1. Rice
2. Portia Sue
3. Teaches

4. Terrapin
5. Soft
6. Edgar
7. Bradshaw
8. Snowball
9. Cord
10. McCall
11. Methodist
12. Green
13. Pampered

202. Mrs. Frisby and the Rats of NIMH (by Robert O'Brien)

Across

1. Mrs. Frisby is a . . . .
2. The farmer, Mr. . . . .
3. The youngest daughter.
4. The sick son.
5. The family lives in an underground house beneath a . . . garden.
6. The farmer's cat.
7. What does Mrs. Frisby worry about?
8. The rat.
9. Jeremy is a . . . .
10. What kind of mice are they?
11. Who does the owl suggest she visit?
12. Under where did the rats live?
13. Characteristic of the rats.
14. What is NIMH?
15. The rats also became this.
16. The rats were in one.
17. How many are in a group?
18. A valley.

Down

1. Her dead husband.
2. The biggest, most handsome child.

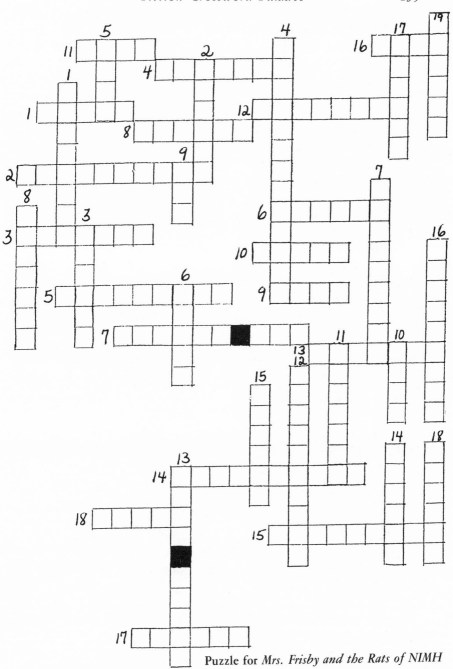

Puzzle for *Mrs. Frisby and the Rats of NIMH*

3. The oldest daughter.
4. The youngest son is a . . . , a person who thinks he is always sick.
5. Mrs. Frisby goes to see someone about medicine, Mr. . . . .
6. The man in #5 Down lives in a . . . wall.
7. The youngest son is ill with . . . .
8. A neurologist.
9. Who does the crow take her to see?
10. The place where the rats have been.
11. What is plowing up the land?
12. What made the rats wise?
13. What did rats become?
14. The rats' guard.
15. Who guards the rats' door?
16. She wants to see a rat.
17. The chief engineer.
18. "The toy . . . ."
19. Who quit the group?

ANSWERS

Across

1. Mouse
2. Fitzgibbon
3. Cynthia
4. Timothy
5. Vegetable
6. Dragon
7. Moving day
8. Brutus
9. Crow
10. Field
11. Rats
12. Rosebush
13. Strange
14. Laboratory
15. Inventive
16. Maze
17. Twenty
18. Thorn

Down

1. Jonathan
2. Martin
3. Teresa
4. Hypochondriac
5. Ages
6. Brick
7. Pneumonia
8. Schultz
9. Owl
10. NIMH
11. Tractor
12. Injections
13. Long-lived
14. Justin
15. Sentry
16. Nicodemus
17. Arthur
18. Tinker
19. Jenner

203. *Up a Road Slowly (by Irene Hunt)*

Across

1. The heroine's father is one.
2. A story of . . . .
3. Her aunt's profession.
4. The boy.
5. The prettiest girl.
6. The oldest girl.
7. Laura wears his ring.
8. Laura's baby.
9. The aunt's sweetheart is a literature authority.
10. What does Julie want to do?
11. Alicia's present.

Down

1. Her brother.
2. How many rooms in her aunt's house?
3. What else is wrong with her uncle?
4. The girl.
5. The oldest boy.
6. The tallest kid.
7. Le Vieux Corbeau.
8. Laura's high school teacher.
9. Her aunt's sweetheart.
10. Her aunt's friend is buying a house.
11. What her father brought to the birthday party.
12. The father's birthday container.

ANSWERS

Across

1. Professor
2. Growing up
3. Teacher
4. Danny Trevort
5. Lottie
6. Elsie Devers
7. Bill Strohmer
8. Julie
9. Russian
10. Write
11. Poems

Down

1. Christopher
2. Twelve

Puzzle for *Up a Road Slowly*

3. Liar
4. Carlotta Berry
5. Jimmy Ferris
6. Chris
7. Wine

8. Allison
9. Jonathan Eltwing
10. Merridan
11. Silver pen
12. Leather box

204. A Visit to William Blake's Inn (by Nancy Willard)

Across

1. Who runs the imaginary inn?
2. The inn is staffed by two . . . .
3. Who shows visitors to their rooms?
4. One of the guests is the man in a hat.
5. Another of the guests, two . . . flowers.
6. How do they get to the inn?
7. What color room do the sunflowers move into?
8. What does the King of Cats order?
9. What does the tiger ask for?
10. "Poems for innocent and . . . travelers."
11. How many years ago did Blake live?
12. This is a book of . . . .
13. The Marmalade man mends us.
14. "In the forest of the . . . ."

Down

1. The inn is staffed by two . . . .
2. They (Down #1) do what?
3. They (Across #2) do what?
4. What do the angels shake?
5. Another guest.
6. What does the wise cow enjoy?
7. Where does Blake lead a walk?
8. When they come home, what does Blake ask for?
9. What soothes the guests?
10. The King of Cats doesn't want his wife . . . .

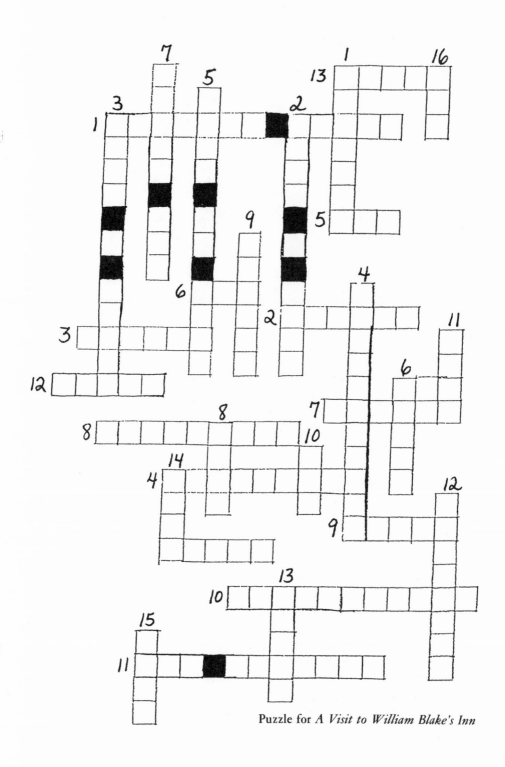

Puzzle for *A Visit to William Blake's Inn*

11. The sunflowers want a room with a . . . .
12. "could frame thy fearful . . . ."
13. What did William Blake also do?
14. The sun and the . . . .
15. "How far? said the . . . ."
16. "What immortal. . . ."

ANSWERS

Across

1. William Blake
2. Angels
3. Rabbit
4. Marmalade
5. Sun
6. Car
7. Yellow
8. Breakfast
9. Story
10. Experienced
11. Two hundred
12. Poems
13. Dance
14. Night

Down

1. Dragons

2. Brew & bake
3. Wash & shake
4. Featherbeds
5. King of cats
6. Cloud
7. Milky way
8. Fire
9. Circus
10. Fat
11. View
12. Symmetry
13. Paint
14. Moon
15. Star
16. Eye

205. *The Witch of Blackbird Pond (by Elizabeth Speare)*

Across

1. Heroine of story.
2. The captain's home.
3. The captain's son.
4. Where does the captain's family go in the winter?
5. He is going to study under Reverend Bulkeley.
6. Era of history.

7. Relative in Connecticut.
8. How many women are aboard the ship?
9. Heroine jumps into the water to get it.
10. Holbrook is going to study with him.
11. Her cloak.
12. Bulkeley is a scholar in this area.
13. Heroine's family owned one hundred of them.
14. The aunt lives on this street.
15. A cousin.
16. Kit's parents died there.

Down.

1. Heroine comes from . . . .
2. Genre of book.
3. Kit is going to settle in . . . .
4. The brigantine ship.
5. The place where heroine feels free.
6. Heroine's first impression of Connecticut.
7. Her home.
8. The aunt.
9. How many days it took for the ship to go from Saybrook to Wethersfield.
10. Aunt.
11. A cousin.
12. The girls make Kit a dress.
13. What Mercy does.
14. After jumping into the water, Kit changes into a dress.

ANSWERS

Across

1. Kit Tyler
2. Saybrook
3. Nathaniel Eaton
4. West Indies
5. Holbrook
6. Puritan
7. Aunt
8. Two
9. Doll
10. Bulkeley
11. Scarlet
12. Medicine
13. Slaves
14. High
15. Judith
16. Antigua

Puzzle for *The Witch of Blackbird Pond*

Down

1. Caribbean
2. Historical fiction
3. Wethersfield
4. Dolphin
5. Meadows
6. Bleak
7. Barbados
8. Mistress Wood
9. Nine
10. Rachel
11. Mercy
12. Calico
13. Teach
14. Green

206. Frankenstein (by Mary Shelley)

Across

1. The narrator.
2. What does Frankenstein create?
3. Victor's mother.
4. His mother dies of scarlet . . . .
5. Victor's father.
6. The narrator's sister.
7. A natural philosophy professor.
8. He is exiled by the French government.
9. The son of the exiled man.
10. The son's fiancée.
11. The expedition becomes stranded by this.
12. Victor hopes to overcome this.
13. Victor knew nothing about his monster for years.
14. Where had the monster gone?
15. The monster learns of where he came from.
16. The monster seeks Victor for a . . . .
17. Shelley uses this device.
18. Letters sent to Mrs. Saville.
19. The atmosphere.
20. The monster always knows where his creator . . . .
21. Where the monster is created.

Down

1. What does he discover?
2. Where is the expedition?

Puzzle for *Frankenstein*

3. Victor's brother.
4. Victor's brother who is killed by the monster.
5. Victor's closest friend who is also killed by the monster.
6. She is adopted by the family, and is accused of murdering William.
7. Victor's wife.
8. Victor goes to this university.
9. The daughter of the exiled man.
10. Victor collected these.
11. What happens to Frankenstein?
12. What does the monster plan to make?
13. What does the monster plan to do to himself?
14. What does happen to the monster?
15. Walton gathers the crew in . . . years.
16. The monster's coloring.
17. Describes the genre.
18. Also describes the genre.

ANSWERS

Across

1. Robert Walton
2. Monster
3. Caroline
4. Fever
5. Alphonse
6. Margaret Saville
7. M. Krempe
8. De Lacey
9. Felix
10. Safie
11. Ice
12. Death
13. Two
14. Shack
15. Journal
16. Favor
17. Letter
18. England
19. Eerie
20. Is
21. Lab

Down

1. Victor Frankenstein
2. Arctic
3. Ernest
4. William
5. Henry Clerval
6. Justine Moritz
7. Elizabeth Lavenza
8. Ingolstadt
9. Agatha
10. Cadavers
11. Dies
12. Bier
13. Burn
14. Lost
15. Six
16. Yellow
17. Unusual
18. Strange

INDEX

Items are indexed to entry number, not page number.

151